Guide-Lines and God-Lines for Facing Cancer

Mind, Body and Faith Connections

Marvyl Loree Patton

LANGMARC PUBLISHING • SAN ANTONIO, TX.

Guide-Lines and God-Lines for Facing Cancer

Mind, Body and Faith Connections

By Marvyl Loree Patton

Scripture taken from the HOLY BIBLE
KING JAMES VERSION
NEW INTERNATIONAL VERSION
Copyright © 1973, 1978, 1984 International Bible Society.
Used by permission of Zondervan Bible Publishers.

Editor: Renée Hermanson
Cover Design: Michael Qualben
Text Illustrations: Susan Q. Reue

Published by LangMarc Publishing
Box 33817, San Antonio, TX 78265

Library of Congress Cataloging-in-Publication Data

Patton, Marvyl Loree 1923-
   Guide-lines and God-lines for facing cancer : mind, body, and
faith connections/ Marvyl Loree Patton.
      p.   cm.
   Includes biographical references and index.
   ISBN 1-880292-12-2 : $13.95
   1. Patton, Marvyl Loree, 1923---Health. 2. Lymphoma--Patients--
United States--Biography. 3. Cancer--Religious aspects-Christian-
ity.   I. Title.
RC280.L9P386 1994
362. 1'9699442--dc20
[B]   94-26046
                                                          CIP

Comments from Readers

"This is the book to read when you think you have exhausted all your resources. If you are wise enough to read it, you will find answers to life's most difficult questions. In it lies the help we all need. Don't wait until you are desperate. Read it now."
—*Bernie Siegel, M.D.*, Woodbridge, CT.
Author of *Peace, Love and Healing; How to Survive Between Office Appointments;* and *Love, Medicine and Miracles*

"Marvyl's account of her cancer is an open window to her soul. It is accurate, insightful and inspiring without being self-absorbed. Marvyl steps outside of herself and makes objective observations. Other times we see her from the inside, dealing with the personal nightmare of cancer. Her cancer is described as a hellish adversary against which she fights with all her strength, and it is also a 'friend' with whom she is forever yoked. This friend provides incredible opportunities for self-discovery, for deepened faith and for ministry. Marvyl's faith is not rhetoric! It has been tested by fire. Her life is a witness to God's sufficiency and grace." —*Thomas B. Anderson*, Pastor
Community Covenant Church, Shawnee, Kansas

"This book is an inspiration to me. In spite of describing numerous life-threatening complications of cancer, it is a joy to read and a meaningful gift to anyone who has cancer or other chronic pain condition. It defines and describes the benefits of self-regulation strategies…such as imagery, in valid and practical ways. Her description of her "last" scuba-diving trip is priceless.   —*Karen Olness*, M.D.
Professor of Pediatrics, Family Medicine and International Health
Case Western Reserve University, Cleveland, Ohio

"This book addresses cancer by showing that there is a brave and bitter struggle to cancer, but that by the use of humor and faith, patients can overcome even some of the most adverse problems. Looking forward to life is one of the most important ingredients in the care of patients with cancer and to help them survive with better quality of life. A very enjoyable book; all cancer patients should have the opportunity to see cancer through Marvyl's eyes."   —*Barbara J. Bowers*, M.D.
Oncologic Consultants, PA., Minneapolis, MN

"Talking about hope, survival and what could be expected, discussing options, alternatives and variations . . . truly a source of inspiration... a snowball that becomes an avalanche of things showing God's involvement and guidance."
—*Bob Otto*, Waseca, MN, Cancer Patient

"Marvyl reaches out to those living with cancer and offers hope and encouragement while inspiring them not only to embrace life, but to search for its meaning. She challenges them to survive, not only physically, but also spiritually; she reminds all of us to pay attention to the ways of the spirit."
—*Charli Johnson*, Support Service Coordinator
North Memorial Medical Center, Service and Rehabilitation,
American Cancer Society, Minnesota Division

"Testimonials from those 'who have been there' are very powerful for someone struggling with a diagnosis of cancer. Marvyl inspires in a manner that exemplifies her life, especially her battle with cancer; faith-filled and from the heart!"
—*Sharol Anderson*, BSN, RN, OCN
Oncology Patient Education, North Cancer Center, Minneapolis

"Marvyl's story is about the strength of the human spirit, the power of love and the possibility of gaining victory over one of life's greatest obstacles. Led by a deep faith in God and guided by a strong belief in self-empowerment, Marvyl describes how you can learn to live with cancer and discover the transcendent power of service to others. Her message is clear: you cannot only survive cancer—you can thrive!"
Judy Ireland, Director
Service and Rehabilitation
American Cancer Society, Minnesota Division, Inc.

"An inspiration to all ages, Marvyl has touched our community with her tireless gifts that are deeply rooted in her faith."
—*John E. Howl*, Retirement Community Administrator

"The imagery exercises are wonderful. I've done some imagery before, but nothing like this. There is so little written on imagery for the lay person. There is a wider audience of people who are interested in pain control." —*A Patient*

Dedication

To all those friends whose names are mentioned in my book, I give thanks for whatever your role in sustaining me.

This story of how God reached to me when I have reached toward him is the legacy I would like to leave for my grandchildren: Mara, Chris, Ben, Freddy, Eric, David, Mary, and Andy. Thanks to my husband, my family, my doctors, my nurses, my pastors, and my friends for helping me to continue finding joy in life.

Contents

Guide-Lines and God-Lines

Charts and Lists

Foreword

More than 20 years of living with cancer and still counting. Continual setbacks requiring treatment and hospitalizations, and yet still spirited. Increasing limitations to comfort and mobility, and yet still determined. This is Marvyl Patton, cancer survivor par excellence.

I have known Marvyl for 16 of those years and can attest to the fact that she finds fullness in life regardless of her circumstances. This is her story, chronicling life since receiving a cancer diagnosis in 1973. Through the use of journal entries, she recalls the pains and joys, the peaks and valleys of this difficult and arduous journey. Marvyl tells it as she lives it—with a peace and serenity that comes from her strong faith in a loving God. Readers gain a new appreciation of what it means to live with a chronic illness.

Marvyl's story weaves together the medical facts about her type of cancer, its treatment and side effects, an understanding of its psychological impact and spiritual relevance. She embraces a wholeness of life by meeting her challenges with a limitless spirit, questioning mind and loving heart.

Guide-Lines and God-Lines vividly portrays the real day-to-day problems encountered by people with cancer. The book does not gloss over or minimize the magnitude of these problems—it addresses them head on. With humor and creativity, Marvyl questions the why, how and when of her predicaments. She describes how to be one's own advocate, and she urges readers to build a support network for when the going gets tough.

This book is unique. It is hopeful and inspirational. It shows that regardless of the gravity of a situation, a person should have choices. It calls for risk taking, attitude adjustment and reassessment of life's values. Marvyl shows readers how to put cancer in its place. In spite of her numerous setbacks and limitations, she views herself not as a cancer patient but as a person who happens to have cancer. Perhaps of all the messages conveyed in this book, the one that is most significant for us to recognize is that life is a gift that needs to be celebrated moment by moment.

Judi Johnson, Ph.D., RN, FAAN
"I Can Cope"—Co-author of a patient education program
adopted by the American Cancer Society
I Can Cope: Staying Healthy With Cancer, Co-author

About the Author

Marvyl Patton, a former social worker, a wife, mother and grandmother, is an educator and innovator with drive and determination that has proven that the human spirit need not be squelched by illness and pain. Now enclosed in a body brace, she is eager to share her story of not only surviving cancer, but of learning to accommodate her growing limitations without compromising her daily mission to help herself and others. She is generous with her love and devotion to her family and friends—and now to you, the reader.

The consummate volunteer, Marvyl was active in scouting, school activities, church, choir, politics and classes for adults and children. She helped organize groups such as Make Today Count and Hospice, verified the value of the I Can Cope educational program in small hospitals as well as large hospitals. She remains a leader in the work of the American Cancer Society. She writes newsletters, materials and handbooks for cancer patients and their families and has been an indefatigable speaker at and organizer of educational seminars and meetings for patients, families of patients and professionals to the patients. Marvyl has been honored for her service and courage at the local, state and national levels, but she always considered parenting, "grandparenting" and family life her top priority and her greatest honor.

After earning her Masters in Social Work at the University of Minnesota, Marvyl was a case worker for disturbed children. Later she taught in the Graduate School of Social Work and also taught in the horticulture department of the University Agricultural Branch in Waseca.

A native of Mason City, Iowa, she and her husband, Bill, a lawyer, lived most of their married life in Waseca, Minnesota. They now reside in Minneapolis.

Introduction

If you reviewed my history over the past 20 years, you might expect me to be a frail little wisp about to expire, or a tough and stable old elephant. Life has hung on the scales, tipping toward my extinction many times. I have filled several journals and files with notes and writings about my life with cancer. The files are not arranged neatly in my desk drawer, but stacked in a hospital wash basin at the foot of my desk. As I look through them, I am aware of the tortuous path of disease.

Yet only some parts of it have been horrible. There also have been God-given joys. There were mountain top vistas of beauty as well as difficult valleys. A nationally-known doctor, speaking to a room full of health professionals, was asked whether faith made any difference in how one lived with cancer.

"Absolutely not," he said.

I am shouting in disagreement!

Bookstores and magazines are full of dramatic personal accounts of people with cancer. Some live, others die. Some find joy, others, anguish. What makes the difference? It is more than medical treatment. It is more than attitude. Everyone's life is determined, in part, by things over which we have no control—both good opportunities and unfortunate happenings: Chances. Making choices about the chances directed the course of my life. In all chances and choices God led me.

Good medical care needs no explanation or validation.

Mind/body relationship and its use does need further documentation to convince both medical and lay people of its influence on health and comfort.

Faith in God provided insight, hope and new perspectives—given sometimes at the time I asked, sometimes much later, but always in a way that surprised, humbled and awed me, and left me certain of His presence. His guidance has been unequivocal and powerful.

In telling my story, I concentrate on: (1) Times when I saw that faith in God made a difference. I have been challenged on my statement that faith has the power to turn tragedies to treasures, but I found that it did. (2) Situations where I was aware that self-regulation strategies, or choices of mind and emotion, affected my progress and adjustment to disease. Pain and illness such as cancer are best treated by a wise combination of medical and self help. Learning to use journaling, imagery, distraction, music, celebrations, exercise, relaxation and gratitude can be improved upon with practice. (3) Knowledge and understanding provided more courage, patience and hope than I would have found if I denied my need to learn. These three provided me with the choice of living with hope and happiness, rather than with anger and anguish during the trials of illness.

I hope my book will be helpful for many new patients, but especially for those who will be told there is no cure, only hope for control. That probably means years of new complications surfacing, but there is still life. Following treatment, life rarely returns to "normal," but is fraught with ever-recurring problems and fears. That is not to be viewed as a failure of God, doctors or the patient!

Credibility for the connections between mind and body is building in both medical studies and public media. Reports appear frequently that seem to validate this, but very little has been written from the patient's point of view, describing with illustrations how the methods may be used. Some mistakenly fear that faith and mind contradict the science of medicine. They do not. I believe they are complimentary facets for maintaining a sense of health and well being. All three have been vital to my living well with cancer.

Marvyl

The most important Guide-Line:
Get the best medical care.

The most important God-Line:
Be still and worship your God.

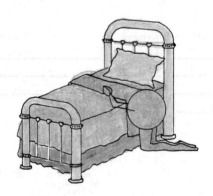

1

They Said It's Not Cancer

"Lie down and lie still," said the tiny Asian woman. I felt her poke a needle between each toe of both feet to inject blue dye. As I attempted to lift my head from the slab-like laboratory table to see what she was doing, she told me, "Wiggle your toes a lot for five minutes to get the dye moving, but don't move anything else. Finding your lymph vessels with this tiny needle is like trying to give an enema to a mosquito."

It was the spring of 1973. I was in a stark, sterile hospital lab. Fifteen feet away lay another patient. We were strangers. We were frightened. We were both newly diagnosed with cancer. Needles, knives and machines explored our bodies in a four-hour procedure called a lymphangiogram. A fine blue line of dye was visible at the top of my foot and the doctor took a small scalpel to make a deep incision, where she injected more dye. As it slowly traveled through my body, it collected in the small lymph nodes to show the medical doctors the extent of my cancer.

The doctor wrote a note to the other patient. When I asked why, she explained that the other patient could neither hear nor speak. An X-ray technician came to my side and positioned a machine over me to check the progress of the dye. As he approached the other patient, the doctor instructed him to write her a note. The technician turned his back and brusquely said, "I don't have time for that." I was appalled. Angry. For many years my father was deaf. I had seen that response when he had not understood the spoken word and proffered pen and paper. With a flip of the hand, people would say, "Oh, it's not that important" and refuse to write. My father had a marvelous sense of humor and infinite patience, but so often he was shut off from communication with people. Could I somehow tell that other patient that I cared and understood? My sign language vocabulary was minimal. I was not even sure I remembered the alphabet. I thought my slight finger movements were unobtrusive as I wiggled my fingers to practice. The other woman, with a look of delighted surprise, began to sign. Both embarrassed and pleased, I signed back to her, "Go slow, I'm dumb." She laughed.

For the next four hours, we were totally engrossed in trying to communicate with the motions of one hand and a turn of the head to lip read. We learned a lot about each other, including diagnosis (hers was thyroid cancer, mine was lymphoma) and how long we'd known (just a few days). We told each other our ages, how many children we had, their ages and names, our husbands' names, jobs, etc. We both came from small towns in Minnesota about sixty miles apart. The doctor commented, "You two have been talking for hours and I haven't the vaguest idea what you've said."

The other patient, whose name was Kathleen, finished with her test first. She was helped off the gurney into a wheelchair. She came over to me, grasped both my hands and with her lips she said silently, "Thank you and good luck." I repeated the silent phrase.

I realized then how the moments of fear and pain had flown by, replaced by an amazing new friendship. Across that chasm of distance, silence and ignorance, we were able to share our fear and reach out to each other. How little we needed to know to help each other! What a beautiful experience to come out of such ominous circumstances! We touched in a way that remained with us for the rest of our lives. Letters and visits continued for years after treatment. What if the preoccupation with discomfort had prevented me from recognizing the beauty in that experience! I must pay attention to God's ways of showing love.

I was a robust and healthy mother of four children and wife of a busy attorney in the rural community of Waseca, Minnesota. In this bustling and progressive town, I participated in advisory committees for the high school and the college and for the retarded in our community. I played golf and bridge. I sang in the church choir and taught Sunday School. I also did wifely things like ironing a stack of clean clothes each week before the creation of permanent press.

Three years before this lymphangiogram episode, I felt a tug in my groin and reached down to see what it was. "My goodness, there is a lump there," I thought. I went to the doctor the very next day.

"Hmmm, probably a small hernia. We'll watch it. I'm sure it's nothing malignant," he reassured me.

A year later, I consulted an orthopedic specialist about pain in my hip and in my foot. He examined my foot, X-rayed my hip and felt the lump still present in my groin. He said a benign growth on a nerve between the toes, called a Morton's neuroma, caused the foot pain. He prescribed a pad to wear inside my shoe, but did nothing about the lump.

Thanksgiving week 1972 was a full one with all of the family home. Paul, 22, was working in Minneapolis. Dan, 20, was in college. Patti, 17, and Bob, 15, were in high school. Also with us were my husband's mother and our new "daughter," Sachiko, a Rotary exchange student from Japan. On Saturday night, after the big holiday, I got up shortly after going to bed. I felt awful; I vomited, had diarrhea and passed out. I came to with severe abdominal pain and had trouble breathing. Bill called for an ambulance. As I was being carried out on the stretcher, my tongue felt too big for my mouth, and I struggled to breathe.

At the hospital, I was placed in the intensive care unit. My heart was erratic; I had respiratory congestion and a vaginal discharge of yellowish red fluid. All my systems were reacting to some strange "bug." First, they checked me for a possible heart attack, then for some tropical disease. A 24-hour jug of urine was sent off to California to test for some rare form of cancer. Two more doctors checked the lump in the groin. "Not malignant," they said, "probably acute gastroenteritis."

Sachiko's gift to me: Trust

During that week-long hospitalization, Sachiko came every day for a visit. Later, I learned it is a custom for young Japanese girls to spend hours discussing the most minute details of friendships with their mothers, but to hide feelings from their fathers. What a sobering thought it was to realize that if I had not been in the hospital, I probably would not have taken time to spend such lengthy hours in discussion, nor would I have realized the importance of that time to her. As her American "mother," I felt honored that she *wanted* to discuss so many things with me, at an age when my own children were asserting their independence from our parental viewpoints.

After a week of monitoring and testing, I was discharged with no further diagnosis. The lump in my groin pulled occasionally, but seemed of little consequence. Life went on.

Sachiko's greatest wish in coming to America was to see Disney World, so we made plans to keep her with us an extra month for a family trip to Florida. Every member of our family was into swimming and underwater diving, so water sports were to be part of our Florida trip. During the winter months, I had accompanied Sachiko to the university's indoor pool until she lost a little of her fear of water. On the drive to Florida, I was tired and my hips ached. In the morning and evening I walked, doing a high "goose step" to relieve the aching. After we saw all of Disney World, our college son, Dan, met us for a week in the Florida Keys, where we snorkeled and went scuba diving.

One memorable day we went on a large dive boat in Pennekamp Underwater Park. Sachiko chose to stay on board. She watched as we snorkeled several hundred feet away from the boat to a reef that was barely covered by water. As the family marveled at the wondrous beauty under water, I heard Sachiko call to me. "Mom, I've decided to go in. If I don't do it now, maybe I will never have another chance. Will you take me?" Still unable to swim, she was bouyed up with a life jacket. Bravely she placed her hand in mine, and we entered the 30-feet-deep water. With a fearful trust, she hung on tightly. We snorkeled to the reef where it was shallow enough for her to stand up. I admired her courage in taking a risk—a quality I would need a lot of in the months to come.

I enjoyed the trip in spite of the mysterious aches and fatigue. I did not even look at the lump until I was back home in front of our full-length mirror. The little walnut size lump had grown to golf ball size. Back to the doctor, who recommended then that I go to "Mecca to the East," a jocular term we used for Mayo Clinic. After three days of examinations and tests, doctors held a conference and invited me to attend. We sat around a long table, four doctors and me. The gynecologist in charge said,

"Four doctors have seen that lump and felt it was benign. Now let's see what five, six, seven and eight think."

"A small hernia"

"A cyst"

"A swollen node"

"We don't know. But we don't think you should be discharged until we find out."

"I'll operate on Monday."

Meekly, I said, "OK."

Easter 1973

On Easter Sunday morning, I was in the church choir as we gathered downstairs to practice before the processional. The minister came to lead us in prayer.

"Gather round Marvyl," he said. "She is going in for surgery tomorrow. Gather closer so you are touching her." Then he prayed.

That afternoon we drove 57 miles to Rochester, Minnesota, where I entered St. Mary's Hospital. A "candy striper" came by that evening and noticed what I was reading. "Everyone is reading the Bible tonight," she said. I felt I was in a safe place. My biggest concern was that all this fuss was over nothing, that my lump was probably something simple and embarrassing like an infected hair.

Next morning, an aide wheeled me to a small room where I waited by myself. People went by the door, more people went by, and still more. I waited. The plan was to biopsy the lump, do a pelvic exam under anesthesia and possibly remove my uterus. I almost hoped they had forgotten me.

After surgery, my foggy mind struggled out of anesthetic sleep. I saw three surgeons enter my room and come to my bedside. They were still in "scrubs," with masks dangling around their necks. Without waiting for them, I spoke first.

"What did you take out?"

"We took out a mass of lymph nodes."

Expectantly, I asked, "Were they benign?"

All three shook their heads in unison and the chief gynecological surgeon responded,

"No, Mrs. Patton, they are malignant. Tomorrow we'll put you under the linear accelerator."

I could scarcely grasp what he was telling me. I looked at my family gathered around me. We were all silenced by fear. As I looked beyond them out the window, I saw a giant evergreen tree, each little branch pointing upward. Its symbolism was clear to me; I must look up, look up to God. There I would find solace amidst what was happening. There I would find help for what was happening. I knew God could be my guide. That realization was so powerful it almost erased my fear—but not quite.

I took a deep breath and asked, "What is a linear accelerator?" They explained. But I pleaded, "Please, not tomorrow. I hurt too much. Give me a little more time."

Further tests were necessary to determine how extensively the malignancy had spread. The next day I was in a wheelchair, hunched over by pain from the seven-inch incision in my groin. First they did a liver scan. As the technician injected dye into my arm, he explained it would give me a flushed warm feeling. I might even feel warm and wet as though I had urinated, but I was not to worry about that. "It just feels that way," he said. He pushed on my abdomen with padded paddles, and a few tears seeped out and ran down my cheeks.

"What's the matter, honey, am I hurting you?"

"No, it's just so hard to learn I have cancer."

In a soft, sympathetic voice he said, "I'm sure it is. When I'm through, would you like to sit here a few minutes before you go on to other tests?" He did not stop his test; he did not change the diagnosis, but I remember the compassion and sincerity of his concern given to me by just a few words. I felt numb and uncertain as I continued in and out of many doors where X-rays, blood tests and more assessments were made. At the clinic appointment desk, I was given a sheaf of appointment slips with verbal directions. I felt overwhelmed. How could I ever remember where I was to go? How could this be happening to me?

There was a church directly across from the clinic. Signs invited people in for prayer, a cup of coffee or information about the city. Bill and I went there to pray and again tears flowed down my cheeks. As the years went by, I returned often to that church for a brief respite from medical consultation. There I could see a face that offered only friendship, not more questions and probings.

Treatment begins

At the Curie Pavilion, a therapeutic radiologist sat with me, knee to knee, eye to eye. "Mrs. Patton, you are looking death in the face, but we can treat you and I hope we can help you! I am so glad we did this test for you. It tells us so much more about your disease and what we need to do," he said as he placed the results of the lymphangiogram in a lighted view box. He pointed to white lumps and explained that they were malignant lymph nodes. The nodes normally are small bean size. Mine were swollen and shaped like those gumdrop orange slices. Many were located up and down my spine and in rows radiating down my hips.

"Do you mean all of those spots are cancer? How can I have that much cancer in my body and feel as good as I do?" I asked.

"That's why I'm showing these to you," he answered. "The radiation treatment will not be easy, and unless you know what we know, it will be hard for you to understand why we are doing it. You are lucky. If you have to have cancer, this is the best kind to have because it grows slowly. A few years ago we did not have a good way to treat it. Now we have a new machine, a linear accelerator, that offers hope for cure."

I had often passed that door marked "Curie Pavilion." I had wondered about the patients within and felt grateful that whatever was wrong with me, it wasn't cancer. Now I was there. What awaited me?

The room where I waited for my first treatment was attractive with piped-in music and colorful orange and purple chairs. Around the room, two people sat side by side, one the patient and the other a family member or a driver. I couldn't always tell which was which. On the first day, I sat next to a woman who was doing needlepoint. She was from Kansas City. Twelve years ago she had treatment for melanoma and was back for a check-up. I looked at her and I thought, "Wow, melanoma is much more virulent than lymphoma. Maybe there is a chance for me."

A nurse came out of the maze-like hallway and called out "Lin-Ac" and then five names. Five patients

followed her for radiation treatment on the linear accelerator, a brand new machine available at only a few
cancer centers in the United States during those years
(1970s). Among the patients in my "Lin-Ac" group
were a young man from India with a brain tumor, a 96-
year-old man who flew in from Texas each week, a
nurse from Michigan, and a young child. We became
friends during that brief waiting time, and I wondered
what happened to each of them after the treatment
phase was over. Once when the machine broke down,
30 patients waited all day while a technician flew in
from California to make the necessary repairs. Before
the day was over, all of us got our radiation treatments.
I was impressed.

I understood that the underground site and the
large heavy doors separating the treatment room from
all else were preventive measures—to safeguard against
radiation leaking out. I lay nude on a "bed" while a
physician and nurse marked my body with tattoos. To
protect vital organs from the radiation beams, they
positioned lead shields on a plastic shelf between my
body and the big machine that hovered over me. They
closed the heavy doors behind them, leaving me alone
and naked. The monster above me began to hum, but I
felt nothing. The treatment lasted only a couple of minutes. I knew I was being watched on a TV screen. I
didn't think it was a very good show.

Contrasts in attitudes toward patients

With a big smile and a hand extended to greet me,
the therapeutic radiologist met with me each week to
talk about my radiation treatments. He made me feel
special by including me in plans for my care. He answered my questions. I felt he was a man I could trust,
and I smiled as he walked away down the hall with his
cocky little strut. The treatment plan was to give me 27

radiation treatments on the linear accelerator. Nine days of radiation, then three weeks of rest to let my cells recuperate. Repeating this cycle three times took most of the summer months.

What a contrast there was among the various physicians who were part of my medical team. One treated me with indifference, looked out the window while I was talking, wrote notes without comment, shared as little information as possible, and smoothly evaded my questions. One day as he hurried out the door, I called him back. He looked surprised when I said, "I need to talk. Sit down and answer my questions." He did, but on the way home I realized that he had avoided or belittled my questions. I felt angry and insecure. Eventually, I asked to see a different doctor.

One day while under the linear accelerator, a very large brown envelope was slipped under my body. Kodak was developing a new type of film so that X-rays and Lin-Ac treatment could be done at the same time. (Two years later it was satisfying to know I had been part of an experiment that worked.) Another time, just as I was about to go into the treatment room, I had a tachycardia attack. My heartbeat jumped to 140 beats per minute. When I asked the physician if this mattered, his reply was, "Not unless it stops my machine."

Soon side effects appeared. Diarrhea and nausea caused me to lose 25 pounds. I lost all pubic hair, labial tissues become black and "weepy," then became very thick, like elephant skin. My inner thighs were blackened almost to the knees. A special lotion and sitz baths helped, but neither the doctors nor I expected the serious long-lasting effects I experienced from the radiation treatments.

I developed repeated episodes of phlebitis (blood clots) in the right leg. Each day I wrapped my leg in an ace bandage, elevated and hot packed it, but that was a minor inconvenience compared with the importance of getting radiation.

When I broke out in a rash all over my body, I consulted my radiologist. He had prescribed Allopurinol to help my kidneys flush out all the dead cells and sloughed tissue, but now I had an allergic reaction to that drug. The alternative was for me to drink 28 glasses of fluid per day.

"*How* many?" I asked.

"You heard correctly; I said 28. I don't care if it's water, wine, tea, whatever you like, but you must drink that much to keep the kidneys flushed. Otherwise you risk a kidney infection, and you don't need that complication."

It wasn't long until I was so sated that I could not hold another glass of water to my lips. I filled a quart pitcher with lemonade, put a straw in the spout and sucked as I carried it around, changing to water, tea or pop when it was empty. Six pitchers a day gave me 24 glasses, plus what I drank at meal time made the 28! Sitting on our outdoor patio, I elevated my leg, sipped and read until I could stand it no longer. Then I'd run to the bathroom. Next, refill my pitcher. Rewrap my leg. Repeat. Repeat. Repeat. I read and did macrame while lying there, but I got tired of it and kept trying to bounce back up. I felt like one of those little round-bottom wooden dolls, the ones that won't lie down. A total of eight clots worked their way up my leg. Finally, I got the message: "Lie down, you dumb doll, you can't get up yet."

Strategy for survival: Learn to accept help

Friends frequently asked, "Is there anything I can do to help?"

"Will you drive?" I asked. If they said "yes," I added their name to a list I kept by the telephone. Each afternoon I called a driver for the next day. I left home very early in the morning carrying a pillow, a green and beige afghan my mother made for me, and my "urp" bag (a brown paper sack with green plastic). Blood tests and X-rays came first. If they were OK, I was sent to the Curie Pavilion for another session with the behemoth. Cumulative effects of his hot breath first appeared when I was visiting another patient, and I had to dash to his bathroom to vomit. All the way home, I vomited green bile every 20 minutes. As I pulled the afghan around me, I felt surrounded by my mother's love. At home, vomiting continued with the same frequency, until I fainted. Before the next treatment, the doctor gave me anti-nausea drugs that helped somewhat.

In spite of the side effects, I enjoyed spending days on the road with each different friend and sharing some of our most precious and intimate feelings.

One restless night, as I tossed and turned, I thought of all the people who had been helpful transporting me and bringing in food. Somehow, I saw myself at the back of our church. It became a game to identify people by the backs of their heads and where they were sitting. I recalled a little something about each person and where they fit into the tapestry of my life. I thanked God for each friend and "telepathized" a thank you to them. Some I remembered to verbally thank in the months that followed.

I dropped out of many of my clubs and committees. For years I had directed Girl Scout day camp for over a hundred little girls at Maplewood Park. It was primitive: no water, no plumbing, no electricity. I was proud of the nature guide we had printed, which we called "Whooo Lives Here?" Keeping that park for nature study was important to me, so I was glad I could still help by doing some telephoning for the Maplewood Park committee. I learned to be content with less responsibility and less involvement. I had a new appreciation for being able to contribute through performing less demanding tasks within my energy limits.

One day after returning home from the clinic, I was lying on the couch by our big picture window. I noticed the Hopa crab apple tree in the back yard, profuse with rose-red blossoms. People came to the door with food for the family supper. Someone was running the vacuum cleaner. The children were going about their usual activities. I felt weary and confused. I had cancer, a most dreaded disease. Radiation treatments were doing unusual things to my body. I could do nothing except lie there like a vegetable. My busy schedule used to make so many demands upon my time and energy that I had sometimes wished the world would stop for just a few minutes so I could catch my breath. I would think of that popular song, "Stop the World, I Want to Get Off." My world *had* stopped and let me off. Other people were taking my place. Then a silent voice spoke to me,

"Peace, be still" [Mark 4:39 KJV].

"Be still and know that I am God!" [Psalm 46:10 KJV].

Was God speaking to me? When had I learned those Bible verses? Was that all God wanted me to do at that moment—to be still, to be aware of His presence, to be aware of the beauty before my eyes, to be more aware of loving friends who were doing things for me, to be blessed by my family around me and to be thankful for the excellent medical treatment available to me? Those thoughts changed my perspective from dismay to gratitude. Indeed, I felt blessed!

Life goes on—

Just after my diagnosis, a small announcement appeared in the paper's hospital notices saying that Mrs. Bill Patton was diagnosed with lymphosarcoma and would be having radiation treatments at Rochester.

An acquaintance called me on the phone. She was diagnosed with a similar kind of lymphoma some years ago. She told me about her treatments and her recovery. She called every week to hear how I was doing. I learned and appreciated how helpful it is just to share experiences with someone who has been there, to be heard and understood.

When we first moved to Waseca, I had met Marie. When she told me that she had cancer, I did not know what to say to her, so I said nothing. In fact, I think I turned away and talked with someone else, just because I was at a loss for words. When other people hesitated in talking with me, I tried to put them at ease. I sometimes wondered if I talked too much, but I wanted others to know I needed their conversation. Neither they nor I should have had qualms about discussing cancer.

One day, Rod, our state legislator, and his wife, Janie, invited us to a picnic at their farm. Some other legislators were there, as well as old friends who were active in politics. Sometimes the conversation was political, sometimes about children or other things we had in common. I felt strange and uncertain at that picnic, as if I were a "drop in" from another world. Their concerns, worries and differences of opinion seemed so very unimportant, so minuscule. I felt so far removed from their daily challenges. I was fighting for life.

Since I left for treatment early in the morning, the children got themselves up and off to school. One day, a letter arrived from the school. Before opening it, I smugly thought it was wonderful to have such well-adjusted, intelligent children; a letter from the school usually meant a commendation. I opened the letter and found a request to discuss a matter with the principal. I swallowed my pride and went to the school. Patti and Bob had been arriving late. However, the principal realized their tardiness was very likely a sign of the stress they felt due to their mother's cancer. The school nurse was helpful, too, and I felt grateful for her mothering, even when the kids began calling her "Mom Gallagher."

Acts of love and concern were given to me daily by my family. I treasured their efforts to visit and communicate with me. Neither our son, Paul, nor his girl friend, Lynn, had a car, so they hitchhiked 75 miles from Minneapolis to visit us. Son Dan was in college in Duluth. I will always cherish the homemade card his girl friend, Kathy, sent to me. She drew a picture of the sun and clouds. Inside was this verse:

"We shall go onward together, My God and I;
But if some dark and cumulus cloud should sweep
the sky,
I shall turn 'Son' ward with singing,
For I know,
He will not ask my feet to walk where He cannot
go."

Kathy Dando Turgeon
Quoted by permission

Calling on God's strength to endure

The more I read, the more I realized that Biblical truths are as meaningful today as they were in Bible times. God gives important choices. When we choose to listen and follow, he may not take away problems, but he truly does give strength to endure them and to learn. Often the day's assigned devotional reading was just what I needed. If not, searching until I found something became a small miracle each time. The words were there for me, but I needed to look; then doors were opened.

I found Bible verse after verse that spoke to my situation.

"What does the Lord require of you? To act justly, to love mercy and to walk humbly with your God." [Micah 6:8 NIV]

"They that wait upon the Lord shall renew their strength: They shall mount up with wings as eagles; they shall run, and not be weary; and they shall walk and not faint." [Isaiah 40:31 KJV]

One day my assigned devotional reading was in the book of Job. I read the whole book and reread it many times during that summer. Was I being tested too? Could I be faithful too? Were my troubles anything at all like what Job went through? From my groin to my knees my skin was black from the radiation treatments. I could have shouted for joy when I read that Job's skin turned black, too!

One of the most important lessons I learned from my cancer adventure was that God always provides a way of comfort and peace, but I must look for it and trust it or it will escape unnoticed.

*Do something
you've always wanted to do.*

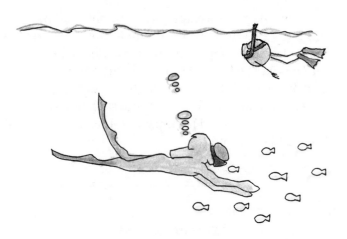

*Enrich your relationships.
Renew your lines of pleasure.*

Mine is Children & Grandchildren - what's Yours?

2

Before
I Die

My two big wishes before I died of cancer were: To walk in the woods once more and to go diving under the water once more.

In the fall of 1973, after radiation treatments were completed, Bill, Patti, Bob and I decided to take one more canoe trip. In that beautiful Northern Minnesota land we could give ourselves completely over to experiencing nature's beauty and our family's togetherness. We could escape clocks, TV, electricity, committees, jobs. Sons Paul and Dan were working for the summer, so they could not accompany us.

The magic started as we drove to the beginning of the trail. Hanging beneath the Sawbill Trail sign was a perfect spiderweb, each thread spangled with dew—so lovely that we stopped to take a picture before driving to our take-off point at Kawishiwi Lake. Pushing off into the misty wilderness was exhilarating! After the

My flower garden— What's yours?

second portage, we were glad to leave behind all the motorboats and people. We were on our own in God's wonderful world, a Garden-of-Eden kind of experience. We found bright red mushrooms and slimy black ones, insect-eating orange-green pitcher plants growing at the edge of Kawasachong Lake. On some of the huge shoreline boulders, we could see faint ripple marks from precambrian waters. In the woods the boulders were covered with thick, gray reindeer moss, soft and spongy under our feet.

Our only creature comforts were what we devised: fire that gave us warmth, cold water baths in the lake, dried food that we carried in packs on our backs, fish we caught and blueberries we picked. A tin cup, hung on a shoestring and tied over a canoe thwart, provided drinking water from the lake. Clothing was minimal: an outfit for cold, one for wet weather, one for hot; tennis shoes for portaging; wool socks and dry shoes for around the evening campfire. Other than the canvas tent, we were not under a roof for two whole weeks.

At each portage, I was given the lightest load to carry. We found high ground on the islands to pitch our tent; we piled stones for campfires and dug our latrine. Sleeping on the ground, which I thoroughly loved to do in the past, was agony for my irradiated body. But I was surviving, and I was in the beautiful, beloved North Woods with my family.

Early one morning Bill and I stood side by side looking out across the misty lake. I soaked up every iota of the experience:

The sights—the ethereal softness of early morning mist merging lake, trees and sky;

The smells—hot coffee in our cups mingled with the fragrance of pine;

The sounds—loons calling, beaver tails slapping, wolves howling, wind whispering in the pines, and often only quiet stillness;

The feelings—joy in creation and visible miracles of God's power.

Was this the last time I would see and hear and feel this way?

As we glided along the lakes and rivers, we sang:

> "My paddle's keen and bright,
> Flashing like silver,
> Swift as the wild goose flight,
> Dip, Dip and Swing."

We were outdoor people who enjoyed nature, camping and roughing it. Before we were married, Bill and I both canoed and had dreamed of a honeymoon in Boundary Waters Canoe Country. Since it was late November when he returned from service after World War II, we skated and skied in 16-below-zero weather on the shores of Lake Minnetonka instead. But we camped and canoed every year after that. Each of our children slept on the ground under canvas before they were a year old. It was our family's time of complete togetherness, without civilization's distractions. Paul, Dan, Patti and Bob learned to love the experience of simple outdoor life and often camped with scouts or church groups as well as with Mom and Dad.

"Thank God anyway"

Smoky was Patti's constant companion and confidant as they romped in the fields and woodlands near home. Smoky was a mixed-breed German shepherd puppy that Patti selected from the Animal Humane Society. The wiggly and lovable pup had a sharp high-pitched bark that hurt the ears, except when she thought she was protecting the family. Strangers walking past our tent in the dark were startled by a low-pitched growl, which did not sound like a small pup with tiny milk teeth.

Sometime after our family canoe adventure, Patti took a day-long trip down the Cannon River with 16 youth from church, and she lost her most precious possession. After a beautiful day on the river, the teenagers beached the canoes and began to load up for the trip home. No one noticed when Smoky, excited by all the commotion, ran into the roadway. A speeding truck hit and crushed the small body as the group watched in horror. Patti was devastated. In her sorrow, she struggled to understand how a loving God could let an innocent puppy die in such a cruel way. She expressed it in a poem. She sought an older friend, Nancy, to console her in her grief. Nancy was a young mother with a small child and an unbounded supply of enthusiasm for life. Nancy listened and talked with Patti. She suggested that Patti "Thank God, anyway."

The words, said with compassion, at first seemed illogical and cruel. Somehow, Patti sensed they were powerful words. Because she trusted Nancy, she sensed that power and she tried it. Doing so enabled her to find some miracles of healing, loving and caring. Theologians describe that as a "leap" of faith. I can think of no better word than that—a trusting, unseeing leap from one's own helplessness to the arms of God—a loving God of power who can make all tragedies triumphant.

I tried it too. I was afraid of cancer. I, too, tried leaping. It did take blind faith. I had first taken that leap long before. It helped me live through and rejoice in the glorious outcome of a marriage once threatened by alcoholism. It helped in loving our teenage son when he rebelled against all I held dear. It helped in a million minor daily trials. Now it was helping me live with cancer. I longed for the comfort of God's love, the joy of His creation, the visible miracles of His healing power. When they didn't appear, I took another leap of faith and said "Thanks God, anyway."

My Second Wish

My wish to experience the Northwoods again was natural. Many of my greatest joys from childhood to my older years were found in nature study. However, to go diving under water before dying is an unusual request for a 51-year-old woman from the heartland of Minnesota.

Nearly ten years earlier, our second son Dan, a husky 13-year-old, announced that he wanted scuba diving lessons at the university pool. He was too young to go unaccompanied by a parent. At first I went just to watch, but scuba is not a solitary sport; safety rules require a buddy system. So Dan's older brother, Paul, and I signed up for lessons, too. The three of us became certified divers and joined the Owatonna Diving Club. It was a family-oriented club and in 1966 it was the largest inland-diving group in the United States. Every weekend, a camping/diving trip was planned to explore the largely unseen world beneath Minnesota lakes and rivers. It was on one such trip to Grindstone Lake in Hinckley that young Dan approached his hard-working father and transmitted diving fever.

On the shore, high above the water, divers assembled their strange regalia. The dive master pumped air into tanks. Divers on the dock took boats to the other side of the lake, where there were steep colorful cliffs. Grindstone is a long deep lake, formerly used heavily by the logging industry. Non-divers, mothers and children casually gathered around various campsites, sunning, talking and playing. Bill sat in the doorway of the family tent, diligently examining abstracts and much too busy and preoccupied to indulge in a frivolous sport.

"Dad, you've just got to see this. Won't you please come to the lake with me?" said a starry-eyed Dan.

Dutifully, Bill put aside his pile of papers and went with his son. Crossing the lake by boat, they pulled onto a rocky shore. Dan gave his father a quick lesson in using the equipment, and they entered the cold, clear water. Visibility under water was 30 to 40 feet. Father and son made a shallow dive and swam easily to a sunken tree. Dan pointed for his father to look up at a large walleye surveying them as they invaded his fishy domain. Bill reached out, nearly grasping the walleye before it slid beyond his hand. Intrigued, Bill began a chase. Dan, laughing, swallowed water as he watched the bizarre sight of his father chasing a walleye pike through the branches of a tree submerged under water. The fish escaped, but father was hooked.

Soon we were a family of certified divers, all except daughter Patti, who did not like being encumbered with all that equipment. She was a speed swimmer, a lifesaver and perfectly content to stand guard while the rest of us went under the water. We watched crappies build nests of small pebbles, lay their eggs, fan them with waving fins and chase away predators in Swenson Lake near Bemidji. Fish, alive and under water, have more color and personality than we imagined.

On one occasion we helped with an underwater search in Clear Lake following a tornado in Waseca. We found bricks, a refrigerator, unbroken light bulbs; and, sadly, Paul found the body of a woman killed by the tornado.

Opportunities came to dive in the Gulf of Mexico, in the calm, clear Florida Keys, in the surging California surf and on the volcanic shoals of Hawaii. It's an indescribable world of color and beauty, of form and movement. Bob asked his older brother Dan, "Why did God make such beauty under water where people can't see it?" Wise Dan said, "For the fish, of course."

In Remission and on to the Cayman Islands

In 1974 the cancer that threatened my life was in remission. We had an opportunity to go to the Cayman Islands in the British West Indies with four good friends from the Owatonna Dive Club. My wish came true!

As we left the Miami airport to fly on a small plane to Grand Cayman, we joked about the plane being small enough to fly with rubber bands. When we arrived, we were surprised by the scrubby growth and trashy appearance of this island paradise. We rented a jeep and found our cottage on the seven-mile beach. The cottage was large enough for six people and came with a native maid, who brought us fresh flowers daily.

A half mile out from Grand Cayman's white sand beach is a coral reef that surrounds and protects the island from high seas. Impaled on the reef are many shipwrecks. Inside the reef, water is calm, with 80 to 100 feet of visibility, and inhabited by tropical fish of every size and hue. The wreck of the ship Balboa lay 60 feet down in the harbor. On the mast we found vibrant yellow tube sponges; on the sides of the ship, parrot fish nibbled for food, and on the ship's ribs, long-nosed butterfly fish probed for a morsel. After the ordeal of cancer, how wonderful it was to feel healthy again and to enjoy such glorious activity.

We rented a dive boat and guide for a trip to the North Bay. Our young guide knew the area as if he had a detailed topographic map in his head. He carried a small rusty hatchet and a spear gun. Our food for the day depended on our catch from the sea. The spaghetti-like strips of raw conch that we piled on soda crackers were as delicious as the boiled lobster and the grilled fish. The water was a clear lime green with large coral heads of antler and elk horn coral creating mazes through which swam a dazzling array of fishes: smiling blue tangs and gray doctor fish, both with scalpels near their tails; stop-and-go-light parrot fish with red, green and yellow circles on their bodies; four-eyed butterflies with their deceptive black spots; fat, friendly overweight groupers, plus endless varieties of purple and green gorgonians and sea whips.

One day we explored Spotts Cove on our own. Our first find was a pale orange flamingo-tongue shell with its colorful spotted mantle extended. It was feeding on a purple sea fan. A clump of a dozen or so white bivalve shells caught our eye near a cleft in the rocks. Peering into the cleft, we were eyeball to eyeball with an octopus.

By what magic of opportunity were we privileged to explore such strange and beautiful sights?

As Bill and I swam out deeper in our scuba gear, we became aware of a strong current pulling us. Looking up, we saw an opening in the coral reef creating a rip tide. Descending under water again, we pulled ourselves along the bottom, rock to rock, scarcely able to make headway against the strong surge. We knew that we could be washed out the channel to the open sea. Hand over hand, we worked our way back along the bottom until, utterly exhausted, we climbed out on the rocky shore.

The last day, we again hired a guide and a dive boat to take us near the turtle farm, an interesting agricultural experiment of underwater farmers, trying to protect and harvest two species of large sea turtles. The water there was milky, full of floating bits of nutrients washed out from the farm operation. Water clarity was poor compared with other parts of the island, but the size and color of the fish were impressive, particularly the blue and green parrot fish that were as big as a man. Pink and lavender anemones were equally large and impressive, like huge succulent chrysanthemums.

The Cayman wall and tunnels were the final destination for this dive. There were only four of us diving, plus guides, both fore and aft. Because of the depths to which we would go, time under water was a critical factor. I hovered at 14 feet to equalize the pressure in my ears. Then I surfaced to add a bit more lead weight to keep me down. I barely made it in the descent time allowed. Sixty feet down we entered a vertical tunnel that was about ten feet in diameter. Coming out on the other end, we were 120 feet deep. We looked down into a blackness that went a thousand feet down. We peered upwards and saw lacy sea fans silhouetted against the water. All around us were small fans and gorgonians, so fragile that when we tried to take them up to the surface, they crumbled from the change in pressure. On ascending, we had to stop 10 minutes to decompress, to let our lungs and bodies adjust to the change in pressure. Bill noticed that his air tank registered empty, so a guide offered Bill air from his "octopus rig." As we ascended and the water pressure lessened, the air in our lungs expanded and Bill did not need the extra air from the guide.

Our flight back to Minnesota was delayed almost 12 hours because of snowstorms in the Midwest. We had more crew than passengers on the big DC-10 going north. The captain alerted us as sky-lab came into view. He then pointed out the comet Kahoutec, which we could see only with peripheral vision. At home all was well. Patti and Bob had "Welcome Home" signs all around the house. What a perfect trip!

Welcome Home!

Be assertive about your care.

Ask questions.
Ignorance and fear blind you.

3

Radiation and Discouragement

After a summer of radiation therapy, I was in remission. Was my cancer cured? The nausea and fatigue were no longer overwhelming me, but I had many questions. Instead of being too ill, too scared, too tired to care, I was beginning to want to be myself again. How much could I do? Would more activity activate more cells to grow? What should I say to my family and friends? They were smothering me with good deeds and care. Sometimes I loved the attention and caring, but sometimes I wanted to assert my independence. Could I? Would they let me? Would it make me worse?

All the people who worked at my hometown hospital knew me, but what did they know about my disease? Could they answer some of my stupid questions? And some that were not so stupid? My cancer specialists were miles away, and there were things I had forgotten to ask. What could a 35-bed community hospital offer to a cancer patient who had spent the summer months in a major cancer center? Were there

experts to answer the questions that arose? Were there
people who could understand my feelings of aloneness
in the big fight? How could my loving family help to
encourage my independence rather than smother me
with solicitude? But sometimes I needed that solicitude. How much? How could I find the confident me I
used to be?

We discovered a neighbor family going through
similar ups and downs with a daughter's leukemia.
Thirteen-year-old Wanda and I became good friends
because we shared instant understanding. Sometimes I
sat with Wanda when her mother ran an errand, and
we laughed at the afternoon "soaps," especially when
actors agonized for days over getting a medical shot for
something or other.

I learned an important survival technique from
Wanda and her mother. At first it puzzled me. Some
days Wanda rode her bike and went to school, while on
other days she was too sick to attend. She took swimming lessons, but on some days she was unable to go. I
wondered why her mother didn't take better care of
Wanda by keeping her at home. What I learned from
Wanda was to LIVE—Live all I can! Do all I can! On
good days be as normal as possible; on bad days get
help.

Activity does not accelerate the cancer. In fact, it
may be this very active life style that helps treatment
work most effectively. Some people stop living when
they get the diagnosis, and the rest of life is indeed a
struggle for them and their family. Others, like Wanda,
live and enjoy all they can. Cancer is different from
most illnesses. It can be, as they say, a "lingering illness." Living and doing definitely creates a happier
time for both patient and family.

One day I attended a lecture about radiation treatment at the University of Minnesota in Waseca. During
the question period, the nursing instructors said they

wished a patient would work with them, so people could get a first-hand report of radiation and chemotherapy treatments. I volunteered and became involved in planning other nursing conferences. I was given an opportunity to tell my experiences, as well as to hear many doctors and nurses talk about various phases of treatment. All these experiences added to my comfort and knowledge.

I began to realize that one of the greatest handicaps for survival was fear and ignorance. Education and information became key ingredients in my survival strategy.

Life Goes On

In 1973 and 1974 we dedicated many weekends to choosing the right college for our daughter, Patti. Most of our college trips were made with me lying on a bed in the back of the station wagon caring for blood clots that continued to form in my right leg. I had white elastic stockings now instead of ace bandages, and that saved a lot of hassle.

The college we chose was one with a strong Christian emphasis. Sensitized as we were to the importance of God's leading, we chose Augustana College in Sioux Falls, South Dakota. We were surprised and pleased at the open and unabashed way the professors and administrators talked about faith in God as being important. Most colleges we visited were far less vocal about acknowledging spiritual issues. We were survivors of two major illnesses: Bill's alcoholism and my cancer. We knew faith was a life line we wanted to hold firmly.

During this remission time, I continued to have contact with Mayo Clinic for check-ups. When Bill's mother was diagnosed with colon cancer, I was grateful for the knowledge I had, so that I could help her through many uncertain times.

Side effects of treatment continued to plague me, specifically poor control of bladder and bowel. It bothered me greatly when I went to Augustana for a Mother and Daughter weekend. There were hundreds of mothers there and restroom lines were long. Sometimes there was nothing I could do but continue to wear my damp clothing. In the room my daughter shared with her roommate, I found posted on their bulletin board some words by Cardinal Newman that helped me tremendously:

"God created me to do Him some definite service. He has committed some work to me which He has not committed to others. I have my mission. I may never know it in this life, but I shall be told it in the next. I am a link in a chain, a bond of connection between persons. He has not created me for naught. I shall do good. I shall do His work. I shall be an angel of peace, a preacher of truth in my own place, while not intending it, if I do but keep His commandments. Therefore I will trust Him. Whatsoever, where ever I am. I can never be thrown away. If I am in sickness, my sickness may serve Him; if I am in sorrow, my sorrow may serve Him. He does nothing in vain. He knows what He is about. He may take away my friends, He may throw me among strangers, He may make me desolate, make my spirits sink, hide my future from me—still He knows what He is about."

Quite frequently, I found a little "love note" taped to the bathroom mirror when I got up in the morning. Usually my husband had already gone to work when I woke up. It gave me joy to know that he still loved me in spite of my current troubles.

One morning, as I started to climb out of bed, there was a sharp shooting pain down my left leg. I eased myself down on the carpet, and I crawled the short distance into the bathroom. I grabbed the counter, pulled myself up and sat down. The shooting pain was there again. I tried to stand up and it shot down my leg again. What was it?

It gradually eased up, as though something stretched out and fell into place, but it recurred throughout the day. When I sat on the couch to read or as I bent my head to wash my hair, pain shot down my leg. As I walked, it caused me to gasp and stumble. The radiologist suspected it was due to adhesions from the radiation. He called me after attending a conference where he learned that massive doses of thyroid might help cartilaginous tissue heal. It was worth trying, so a program was set up to give me graduated doses of Cytomel over a period of time. He said eventually I would become quite hyper: "You will want to climb the walls." The dose was increased time and again, but nothing happened. There was no relief from the pain and no indication of hyperthyroidism.

I consulted with a number of physiatrists in physical medicine who tried different modalities of treatment. The first was heat and massage. Bill woke me each morning by turning on a heat lamp and the TV. I rolled over and watched the morning news as he massaged. It was pleasant but had no effect on the shooting pains.

Next I tried resting the limb and walking with a cane. Our minister saw me coming downstairs to the church choir room using a cane. He expressed such concern that when he asked how I was, I told him. After about three weeks of this, I did not like what I heard myself saying, so I made a conscious decision not to complain. I deliberately tried to phrase my answer to him with positive words.

A Patient Must be Assertive to Survive

Did anyone know how I felt, isolated and alone with my pain? I consulted my local doctor about continued pain in my hip, lumps in my armpits, and a feeling of tiredness and lassitude. The doctor examined me and called Mayo Clinic to set up an appointment. In the mail, I received an appointment card for October 1975, several months away. With new evidence of disease, I was concerned about my ability to help Mom and Dad as they prepared to move from Arkansas back to Iowa. I made a direct call to my Mayo Clinic specialist to explain why I needed to be seen before October. He pointed out that I was not due for evaluation until then. I explained, persistently, that I must be seen now.

"All right, Mrs. Patton, I'll give you 10 minutes of time if you want to come over tomorrow," he said with a sigh.

"That's fine, if in 10 minutes you can tell me I'm OK," I replied.

"Well, we can't set up any sophisticated diagnostic tests that quickly, but come on over and I will see you."

The surprised look on the doctor's face the next morning told me more than his words.

"I'm awfully sorry, Mrs. Patton. I want the radiologist to see you. We will admit you to the hospital this evening and schedule tests to begin tomorrow." I was not scared. I was relieved that I was getting some attention to the symptoms that had been bothering me. I was also a little angry as I thought, "Oh yes, you *can* set up tests right away."

That was probably when I first realized that **a** patient must be assertive to survive.

Hope for control

A surgeon performed a biopsy on the lymph nodes in my armpits. It revealed active cancer growth above the diaphragm. I had not been cured. My prognosis changed from "hope to cure" to "hope for control." My head was scanned. I was advised to give my teeth a daily bath of fluoride gel to prevent radiation damage. I was given a prescription for artificial saliva to keep the digestive tract lubricated. New tattoos divided my body, and I was scheduled for two cobalt radiation treatments per day.

"Don't cut your hair. You'll need whatever is on top to cover the baldness," said the radiation therapist as he explained I would be treated from diaphragm to the top of my ears. In a very short time, hair came out in big clumps whenever I ran my fingers through it. I knew it bothered Bill when he said, "Don't do that!" Strangely, it did not bother me; I thought it was rather funny. I borrowed a blonde wig from a friend and wore it to the grocery store. It felt scratchy and hot and I felt like a fake. My head became shiny bald from the top of the ears down, but there was enough left on top to cover up fairly well, so I discarded the wig.

I got two consecutive treatments with the cobalt machine each day. I was intrigued by a technology that included placing a finger-cot full of rice over the incision in my armpits to scatter the cobalt beams at the right depth. Lead shields were arranged to protect my heart. I felt tired and light-headed, but I did not experience the nausea that I had earlier from abdominal radiation.

A short time later a dimple developed in my breast. I was asked to sign a release for a new procedure, a computerized breast scan. I was placed in a canvas hammock with a hole in it for one breast to poke through. I was lowered into a big vat of water while the scanner went round and round probing each centimeter of breast tissue for a numerical reading that indicated tissue density. Each breast was scanned. Long pages of numbers came out of the machine and were visually examined for a particular numerical pattern. The numbers were converted into a black and white picture. Results showed that a suture from the biopsy had caused an infection that traveled down a milk duct.

Each week I lost weight. When my weight loss totaled 50 pounds, I took my wedding dress out of the plastic bag in the storage closet, where it had been since 1945. My daughter and I had fun modeling it and taking pictures. I bought new slacks and dresses in size 8-10 and I felt that I had regained a slim teenage figure. To my family, however, I looked gaunt.

A Valley—and a Mountain top

One day in 1975, I was scheduled for tests at Mayo Clinic to find what caused the pain in my leg. An electromyogram (EMG) would test nerve to muscle reaction. I climbed up on a table next to a large green monitor that emitted disturbing noises. Electrodes were placed up and down the full length of my leg. Jolts of electricity were given at each site; small jolts in the beginning, gradually getting stronger and causing my leg to jerk and the machine to make louder crackling noises. The next phase involved putting large needles into muscle at various points up and down my leg. Again stronger and stronger electrical current was used. The whole test was frightening and very painful.

All the technicians left the room and I was supposed to get dressed. Alone and in deep pain, I could not climb down from the table. I could not reach my clothes. I waited; no one came in. On this small table in the middle of a small room in this huge clinic complex, I was trapped and no one knew it. I waited and waited. Gradually I eased myself over to where I could reach my clothes. I dressed and left the room. Still no one noticed me.

I felt a kinship with prisoners of war who were tortured. Did I feel sorry for myself? You bet I did! As I hobbled and limped down the long corridor, tears were close. I had cancer again, I'd lost my hair, I'd lost 50 pounds, I walked with a cane. I hurt, I hurt, I hurt.

As I stepped through the heavy door of the Curie Pavilion for radiation treatment, I seemed to hear a God-like voice speaking.

"Marvyl Patton, what do you think you are doing here? Remember the first time you entered this room. Look around you!"

I did remember. I remembered the lady from Kansas City who told me she was there for a check-up following her treatment 12 years ago for melanoma. Could there be that kind of hope for me? As I recalled that moment, I decided, "OK, God, I'll try."

I struck up a conversation with a stranger from Mason City, Iowa, my childhood hometown. This was her first time here, and she was scared. It was her husband who was ill, and he had already gone down that long hall for treatment. His diagnosis had been delayed for two years, much as mine was, and she feared it was "too late." I told her that I had been coming here for two years and had had 30 radiation treatments. About that time her husband came down the hall. She ran to meet him, grabbed his hand and pulled him toward me, saying, "Just look at this lady. She's had 30 treatments of the kind you just had." He looked me up and down from head to toe. I thought he was seeing the cane, the hair loss, the skinniness, the weakness. Before I had a chance to say even one word to him, he said, "Wow! You're beautiful. Just seeing you gives me hope!" I felt a surge of relief as self-pity dropped from my shoulders.

We had each given the other a precious gift.

TENS (Transcutaneous Electrical Nerve Stimulator)

Ice packs and exercises were tried over a period of months. Finally, one therapist suggested we try an experimental procedure—the use of a Transcutaneous Electrical Nerve Stimulator (TENS) which, in theory, blocked the nerve pathways and prevented the pain message from getting through to the brain. The first treatment was given in the clinic, and I hurt so much afterwards that I could hardly get off the therapy table. I had one treatment each day with a therapist in the clinic and then took the machine home to give my own treatment in the evening. Just the *thought* of electric shocks made the treatment unpleasant. The constant tingling while the machine was on was irritating, and when I turned it off my back muscles seemed tight. It hurt. However, almost immediately, I noticed that the pulsing of the TENS unit stimulated the bowel to peristalsis. Since poor bowel function was also a post-radiation problem, I decided it was worthwhile to continue using this strange machine.

The early TENS units were about the size and weight of an old-fashioned tape recorder and fit into a bag I carried on my shoulder. I slipped the electrodes under my clothes and attached them at the base of my spine where they seemed to do the most good. There were three knobs to set: pulse width, frequency and strength. The first time I wore it to church, I sat comfortably for the opening announcements. It was time for a hymn and I stood up. Wow! A jolt of electricity zapped me. After that surprise, I adjusted the controls downward before changing position. Several times a day I put on the electrodes, set the dials and let it pulse away.

While I was having radiation for cancer recurrence during the summer of 1975, we began building a new house. A realtor friend of Bill's had enticed him with the offer to purchase a lot in a new housing development on the golf course. I was not enthusiastic, but perhaps it would be good for us, particularly for my husband. I thought if I did not survive, it would be better for him to be in a new location near the golf course with new activities and things to do. We did a lot of our own work while we were building. Bill was skilled in design and construction. My skill lay in picking up all the lumber scraps and stacking them in a basement bin for later use in the fireplace. After attaching the TENS electrodes to my body, I could leave it on for a few minutes or for several hours while I worked. Eventually the pain lessened, and after about six months I discontinued its use.

Later, I read an article that reported researchers discovered the use of TENS increased the production of endorphins that control the perception of pain. In a similar fashion, acupressure and exercise stimulate endorphins. My doctors concluded that when those lymph nodes next to the spinal column shrank under radiation, they had adhered to the nerves where they exit the spine, thus creating pain. Information and experience at this time were very helpful many years later, when pain again invaded and tried to inhibit and inhabit me.

When the radiation treatments ended, son Paul and I went to Arkansas. We helped Mom and Dad sell, pack and do all the things necessary for them to move back to Iowa. During the next month, the contractors who had been working on our new house were asked to build an office for my husband's new law firm. The same weekend the office moved, we moved into an unfinished house. It was a busy and stressful time. Often I felt frustrated, tired or confused. I became especially concerned when I was unable to remember things such as my phone number or notes I had written. I was upset when I couldn't concentrate on a university lecture we attended. My head hurt. Had cancer moved to my brain? I consulted the oncologist, but he had no explanation for those persistent headaches.

I went back to the radiation therapist. He listened to me with understanding, then consulted his notes. Yes, he knew why. All the hair follicles were zapped by the radiation and were inactive for several months. Now they were beginning to function again so I could expect a lot of prickly, strange feelings in my head.

When my head hurt, it was natural to try to hold it still; that led to a stiff neck. What a relief to hear that simple and logical explanation.

Paul, a computer engineer, had a wise and perceptive answer: "Mom, you're OK. Your head has just had too much input. Your circuits are overloaded."

Depression

The following winter was my time in the pits. The second go-around of treatments had taken every ounce of energy. I hated the big gray marble tower where I went monthly for check-ups. I wanted to kick every shiny slab. I tried to assuage my anger by walking half way around Rochester's Silver Lake, kicking snow chunks.

There were some particularly bad days when everything seemed to require too much effort. Things I normally liked to do took more energy than I could muster. I felt depressed, discouraged, worn out. In desperation one morning, I wrote all of my feelings down on paper. (Now, when I re-read them, I cringe at some of the memories of despair.)

I realized I was in dangerous territory when I did not want to see or talk to anyone. I did not want to wash my hair or take care of myself. I was wallowing in misery. I wrote it all down in columns: How I felt now. How I used to feel. How I wanted to feel. And what I might do about it. When Bill came home that noon, I felt it was risky to show him what I had written, but I desperately wanted to get better. Intellectually, I knew it might help to share my feelings and fears with him, so I asked him to stay a little while and talk with me. He listened. Hesitantly, I showed him my pieces of paper. I had made a chart of my concerns.

AREAS OF CONCERN

TIRED

—*Sometimes I feel not only tired, but fuzzy, in a fog, not quite out of touch, but almost. Only with conscious effort can I focus on the big picture. It is difficult to make decisions. I don't know what I want. I can be easily influenced. I have a "don't care" feeling.*

—*I used to feel very confident, very much OK most of the time. I had physical, mental and emotional limits, but I knew what they were. Now I feel like all three are closing in.*

INERTIA

—*It is hard to get started at anything. It takes a long time to decide to do something, even simple things like washing my hair or going downtown. I postpone or put off all I can. I am reluctant to call on the phone, reluctant to visit friends.*

—*Interaction with people used to be my "talent." I had a seemingly endless supply of energy and enthusiasm. I loved contacts with people, found it easy to relate to people, always reached out, wanted to be where things were happening.*

STAMINA

—*I can't keep up the pace, even a slow one. I have to sleep 9-10-11 hours a night. I hate to undertake anything that requires continuous effort, like a committee. I hate to commit myself to a future activity, even a party.*

—*I used to like getting up; I did not want to miss anything. I had reserve energy to tap when demands were especially heavy. I could keep going and honestly not feel exhausted. Now, only when I'm with my folks and see their inadequacies due to age, do I feel adequate and capable by comparison with them.*

EMOTIONS

—*I feel an emotional flatness, can't even recall the right term for it. Don't feel as exhilarated as I should about something good, like the new house, the kids coming home, etc. I don't feel as sad as I should about the death of a friend.*

—*I used to operate on a much higher plane. I've never had broad mood swings to high peaks and low places, but enjoyment of whatever I did was characteristic.*

MEMORY

—*My short-term memory doesn't work. I forget things like phone numbers, zip codes, abbreviations I made on a note written the night before. Thinking back to what our life was like before cancer seems eons ago.*

—*I've had no trouble with memory before.*

SEX

—*I have no physical drive, sometimes an emotional need, but it seems almost covered up by a physical "blahness." I have recurring vaginal discomfort, burning, swelling, pain, discharge. Touch is painful, washing stings, slacks are tight. I am uncomfortable. I have cramps and tightness in my hips and legs. Infections require the use of medication that hurts so much that tears fill my eyes.*

—*I've always been more passive than aggressive, but I could be easily stimulated. It seems a real effort to try to remember how sex is supposed to feel and to try to recall the right sensations. I can do it, but it really feels as though I have to exert mind over body.*

FLEXIBILITY AND RESILIENCE

—*I would rather not tackle or change plans. I prefer a laissez-faire approach. Most things look or sound like they'd be too much trouble. I have to force myself to try anything.*

—*I used to be willing to try anything. Difficulties and changes in plans were a challenge. When no one else would try, I would. What no one else wanted to do, I'd do.*

COMPREHENSION

—*It is difficult to grasp something new, like a university lecture we attend, like how to set up the fish tank, like how to operate my new sewing machine. Figuring out how to sew curtains, figuring finances, figuring or planning most anything results in headache, weariness and doubt.*

—*I used to be challenged and stimulated by new thought or new activity. I used to feel competent, and even if skeptical, I was intrigued enough to try to understand a new concept. I usually was successful; now I don't even want to try. Buying a new sewing machine was a desperate effort to prove I could still do something.*

PHYSICAL

—*I have headaches much of the time. My back aches mostly at night. I get cramps in my feet, hips and legs while I'm sleeping, walking, or climbing up on a stool. I don't feel well most of the time. I have occasional dizziness. My hair is terrible to manage. We start for a walk, but at the end of a block I am exhausted and head for home.*

—*It used to be that change of activity, exercise, rest, or an occasional aspirin would take care of all aches and ills. I had very few. I could override or compensate for almost anything and feel OK. I liked my qualities of enthusiasm and endurance.*

GUIDELINES FOR WHAT TO DO

—*Rely on the guidance of God and the Holy Spirit.*

—*Accept what I cannot change, but give it a good try.*

—*Try to determine whether exhaustion has physical or mental causes.*

—*Try to determine how much I should push myself, even when I don't feel like it.*

—*Don't complain. (Bill, is it easier to live with a complainer or a zombie?)*

—*Be cheerful, smile, be enthusiastic.*

—*Get at least one something done each day.*

—*Have at least one outside contact every day or two. (It is OK to hole up for a day, but then get out again.)*

—*Get enough rest. Right now my body seems to need it. Accept that as OK.*

—*Try to keep up with a couple of outside commitments such as choir and our church's Ladies Friendly group.*

—*Don't dawdle! Force myself here. Make myself do things and do it quickly. Get going when I decide to do something, visit a friend, or have someone in for coffee, sweep the floor, write a letter.*

I drew a graph to try to show Bill how I felt and to visualize for myself where my highs and lows were. I was afraid he might belittle those awful feelings I was having. Instead, he was supportive and understanding. We talked of how God had led us out of the despair of alcoholism. We recalled the uncertainty and fear we both felt as we drove home from the addiction treatment center after his discharge. How clearly we had felt God's presence then, almost tangible, hovering over us. The awareness then of the *reality* of God in our lives brought tears of awe and gratitude.

That is what we needed now. We both agreed that the first step out of my depression was to rely on that guidance of God and the Holy Spirit.

Dear God,

> *I feel so tired,*
> *My body so out of condition,*
> *So uncertain with my illness*
> > *and its daily manifestations.*

> *How do I get out of it?*
> *Not by sitting and waiting—*
> *I lose time and opportunities.*
> *But by getting going,*
> *By getting up and doing.*
> *That's the way to strengthen*
> > *my body, my spirit, my psyche.*
> *No one else can do that for me.*
> *No one is going to coax me.*
> *No one is going to make me.*

> *Only I can do that for me—*
> *With Your help.*

> > > > *Amen.*

Borrow strength from others.
Give of your strength to others.

Asking for help shows
you have strength
and are taking control.

4

The Mind
Takes Hold

The summer of 1975 was spent traveling again to Rochester for radiation treatment. As before, volunteer drivers provided my transportation. What a day to celebrate when I could finally drive myself to Austin to meet with Kathleen for lunch at a mall restaurant. We hugged and rejoiced at our mutual survival. It was frustrating to try to say all I wanted in sign language. My vocabulary was so limited and interpreting was so slow. I resorted to writing notes. (The day would come when we could spend two hours together and not write, but that would take, in the interim, concentrated effort, lessons and time.)

In the fall I contacted a dear friend, Hilary, who was skilled in sign language. I was eager to learn more. We became so enthusiastic that soon we both took more signing classes at the Faribault School for the Deaf. Our lunch hours at McDonald's were almost riotous fun as we laughed at our mistakes and overcame all shyness about signing. We learned that words like "sex" and "just" are differentiated by the right crook of a finger. We appreciated a special brand of humor as we struggled to make sense of the jokes told by our deaf instructor. Next we undertook the leadership of a Senior Girl Scout Troop, and we taught them to sign. After months of learning and practicing, the troop adopted a junior troop of deaf girls and took them winter camping. One little girl did not want to pull her share of the load as we carried our supplies into camp by toboggan. She plumped herself down in the snow and pulled her stocking cap down over her eyes so she could not "hear" us.

Together, Hilary and I taught signs to the residents of the retirement home where Mom and Dad lived, so Dad might have some friendly communication. We were asked to teach a sign language class in Community Education for parents and teachers of deaf children and for the staff of a group home. The first class in the group home was a thrilling milestone. A very abusive, sometimes violent and difficult young woman gave the staff a great deal of trouble because they could not communicate with her. After we "talked" with her, she ran excitedly all around the home signing, "I have a friend, I have a friend!"

To think that this had all begun on an examining table in a sterile environment at Mayo Clinic.

Make Today Count (MTC)

One afternoon Hilary brought me a magazine article about Orville Kelly, who started Make Today Count as a support group for cancer patients. Orville Kelly's lymphoma was similar to mine. He, too, went through a time of depression after diagnosis. I wrote to him for information. In the pamphlets he sent back to me, the words that struck me were in big print: "DO IT!" Start a support group! I knew I had the skill, experience and training to start a group. I also had the backing of people who could help in the medical community. So I should DO IT.

In a town such as Waseca with its 8,000 people, it was not difficult to know who was ill with cancer or other serious disease. I called all the patients I knew, the nurses and doctors, the social workers and pharmacists. I also contacted the newspaper and radio station. They all came—more than thirty people met in the library. I explained briefly what Make Today Count groups did. Then we went around the table, each one expressing why we needed such a group.

"Should we start a group in the fall?" I asked.

My doctor replied, "Why wait until fall? The iron is hot now!" So we set a time and a place for meetings. Those who objected to using hospital facilities for our meeting place soon learned to view it as a place of comfort and help, rather than a threat to be avoided.

Many good things began to happen in Make Today Count (MTC). We were a diverse group of 20 to 30 people, all with illnesses that altered or threatened life.

Lorraine's 11-year-old son came with her. She'd had a double mastectomy and had inflatable prostheses. She laughingly told us she knew things were well in hand when her son approached her with a hat pin and said, "Mom, do you know what it's like to have a deflated ego?"

Dave and Dave: There were two of them, both with multiple sclerosis. They brought out the best in all of us by competently driving their own cars, managing their wheelchairs by themselves, then using their extra mobility to cart books and boxes for the rest of us.

Ruth lost her vocal cord and a breast in two separate surgeries, but she continued to teach math in high school. Because of her charm and dedication, she never had an instance of disciplinary problems even though she spoke only in a whisper. She had her own house, but she told us she did not live alone; she lived with Jesus. No new prostheses for her, a couple of old nylons rolled up in her bra did very well. She was our most faithful telephone caller; she kept track of us all and really cared when we were sick.

Gert did not dress nor did she go out of the house after her diagnosis. She stayed in bed, face to the wall. She could not be urged out of her shell of fear and despair. Others made well-intentioned efforts to reach her on a professional basis; friends tried, one on one. Finally we coaxed her to come to the group meeting, and it changed her life. Immediately she was no longer alone, the sick one among a big family of healthy ones. Here she was among many who understood and gave her lots of "warm fuzzies." Like her, we were all struggling with serious disease. There was delight and laughter when Lorraine said to her, "We might as well go home and clean those cupboards. We're going to live a while." And Gert did live. She was helpful to her family during the illnesses and deaths of her sister, her mother, and her husband. She wrote articles for our newsletter and was dedicated toward helping other ostomy patients.

Lloyd, who had an ostomy, came from a nearby town. He still conducted his electrical trade in area farms and rarely missed a beat due to his illness. His marvelous wife was deaf, but she was so skilled at lip reading that she could understand conversations going on across the street.

Ewald got up at 4 a.m. to irrigate his colostomy so he would not disturb his family. Close to 80, he was the oldest member in our group.

Hazel was a great survivor. Her surgery was performed in the pioneer days of colostomies with no medical follow up. Through our MTC group she heard about and attended a conference where she amazed the doctors and medical people with the quality of her survival.

Young **Dave**, so good looking in spite of hair loss, was still in high school. He came with his dad or mom or one of his 10 brothers and sisters. Together they found they could say the word "cancer" out loud, and they learned that there was hope for tomorrow. (Dave did recover from leukemia and now, many years later, he is in medical practice.)

Hortense was rather strange in custom and appearance. But she baked us all a cake for a meeting just a week before her death. She said when she brought it in, "For the first time in my life I feel like I really have friends."

Joyce didn't always feel well enough to come, but if we gave her a call before a meeting when we needed refreshments, she'd come with a marvelous assortment of cookies and bars that had been brought to her home. She delighted in being able to contribute.

Lenora was another who liked to contribute food. She was very faithful in her attendance and so good about writing cute little notes with her own unique style of abbreviating words. Her upbeat ways of finding fun were an inspiration.

Vicki, Jeannie's daughter, became part of a study group of children who choose to die in their own home. Our knowledge and understanding of feelings were so enlarged by Jeannie's words, spoken in the accent of her native France. We visited Vicki at home. Several years later, members of her family spoke at a nursing conference to tell others about the rewards of caring for a dying child at home.

Cindy was barely in her twenties and very sick in the hospital with complications from ovarian cancer.

Her devoted young husband fed her small spoonfuls, but hyper-alimentation (tube feeding) became necessary. Visits, encouragement and hope surrounded her from our MTC members. We held a big party with posters, signs and balloons when she came home from the hospital and began recovery. Today, she travels with her husband for business, and for fun she takes karate lessons.

Phyllis: Tears of sorrow flowed during Phyllis' first meeting. She was diagnosed with pancreatic and liver cancer, not a hopeful combination. Her daughter was in Africa serving as a nurse missionary and not due home for another year. Her husband and son were with her to give support. Phyllis continued a full-time job during her treatment. Later she spoke at cancer workshops. Her calm and cheerful manner deeply affected me. Years later when we had moved away, I rarely saw Phyllis, but her notes and the knowledge that she survives give me a lift.

Bernice, a forthright senior citizen, broke the ice for a couple of new people with laryngectomies. One evening as we went around the room introducing ourselves, they hesitantly used their artificial voice boxes. Around the circle, it was Bernice's turn. "Don't be self-conscious about your toys; many of us have artificial playthings," she said with a freeing humor as she bounced her mastectomy prosthesis.

It was our custom at meetings to go around the table sharing our most recent experiences. A young minister carried a burden of despair and guilt over losing his job because of his illness. With MTC members he found instant, sincere support and respect for his skills. It wasn't long before a strong bond glued together our 30 or so members. How much we cared about each other! We shared our mutual limitations. We now had a place to express our daily pain and doubts, which previously many of us had endured alone. If a problem came up between meetings, we knew someone to call. Or, we could "tough it out" until Monday evening when the group would meet again. We had access to sympathetic ears. We shared not only sorrows and joys, but knowledge and ideas that equipped us to cope.

Equally significant, we had access to speakers and films not available to us as individuals. When we had a well-known speaker or medical specialist, our attendance might soar to 75, overflowing the hospital conference room where we met. We became known as a resource for the community. Others called us to ask for information. We developed a library of educational books, research reports, pamphlets, and magazines. We exchanged newsletters with other hospitals and support groups. An enterostomal therapist helped us make a display board of ostomy appliances. Pharmaceutical representatives and the hospital central supply provided samples and booklets about nutrition. Louie, the hospital maintenance man, built us a whole wall of book shelves, and an ex-librarian helped catalog and check out our materials.

We asked a representative group of people to serve as our advisory board to brainstorm ticklish questions, such as what it might do to the group if we said "yes" to mentally ill patients who asked to come to our meetings. The advisory committee helped us decide that our doors were open to anyone who found the meetings beneficial to them, regardless of their condition or illnesses. At the same time we developed a policy of having a specific focus or theme for most meetings. We announced in advance that the next meeting would be about pain, breast cancer, etc. This helped to keep our discussion on track and discouraged rehashing the same stories or getting off on a tangent. Several mentally-handicapped people came to three meetings but decided for themselves that what we had was not for them.

Not all meetings were without anxious moments. While driving into town, I often wondered if anyone would attend. As the group's chairman, I felt responsible if nobody showed up. Attendance was sparse at a few meetings, but I discovered a small group meeting is just as fruitful as when we had a larger turnout. There were times when only one or two of us would go to a patient's hospital room to meet with him or her. I was reminded of Jesus' words, "wherever two or three have been gathered together, I will be in their midst." Before each meeting, I prayed that it would be helpful to someone and that we would be doing God's will in being with each other. It wasn't hard to see the results in my own life, often in unpredictable ways, as we cancer patients interacted with each other.

"Cheer and Chatter"

"Let's make up a little newsletter for each other and for patients in the hospital," Lorraine suggested one day. She had been a patient in a larger hospital elsewhere and found its morning newsletter such a day brightener. We started with a single mimeographed sheet of "one liners," bits of poetry, and weather information or hospital items. Hazel suggested we call it "Cheer and Chatter." From an ostomy group in Nevada we borrowed a sketch of a strong daisy bending to speak to a weaker one and saying, "You'll be up again." We used it as a logo for our newsletter. On the cover's other side we printed a list of resources in the community where various kinds of help were available. Char had artistic skills, and her sketches added interest and vitality to each issue. Others began supplying funny sayings, inspirational bits, and news of medical advances. Some also submitted writings of their own. Our newsletter grew and so did our membership.

To remain vital, cancer support groups must reach out to newer patients. For maintaining group strength over the years, I found these valuable guidelines from the Multiple Sclerosis Society support groups:

1) Share leadership and responsibilities.
2) Broaden the knowledge base with education.
3) Provide fringe benefits, some way to make members feel special.
4) Develop a network of support, methods of maintaining contract.
5) Reach out. Make newcomers feel welcome. Older members give encouragement to new patients and become role models.

Many cancer patients were involved. Sue typed, Ernie kept track of the mailing list, Char sketched, I edited, the hospital furnished a copying machine. Others began to take notice. A representative of the United Way board called to say we were contributing so much to the community that they would help fund us, if we would submit a budget. We obliged. We contacted the Post Office about qualifying for bulk mailings. Fran filled out the forms, sorted the mailings by zip code and delivered them to the post office. A committee stapled and addressed the newsletters with labels made by Ernie. Soon we could afford a commercial printer. Our printing expanded from 50 copies to 500 as new members joined and asked us to send "Cheer and Chatter" to relatives and other patients around the United States. I began to get phone calls and letters from people who wanted to thank us or ask us for help in getting a similar group started. People in nearby towns asked our members to meet with new groups. Like a bunch of mushrooms, ours and other groups sprang up, gaining strength from each other, spreading out and giving and receiving nourishment in ways none of us had foreseen.

One particular day stands out in my mind. Physically I was still thin, weak and hurting. The phone rang. It was a nurse in Nevada who had seen our newsletter and wanted suggestions for starting a group there. The phone rang again. It was a local man inquiring how to help his parents. Another phone call came from a friend who just wanted to know how I was doing. My days began to fill up with purpose and affirmation. How could I help but thank God! However my illness came about, I had found a purpose being where I was and doing what I was doing.

On my next clinic trip for evaluation of my cancer, I no longer was worrying about the outcome. Instead, I experienced a powerful sense of gratitude that God provided me with a purpose and a mission that I had not seen before. God had given me an empty niche that He was helping me fill with work, purpose and rewards beyond anything I'd been able to expect or foresee.

The American Cancer Society

1977: A year went by. I was in remission again, so medical check-ups were spaced every six months instead of three months. Should I, *could* I go back to work to help with the expense of having four children in college in the fall?

After exploring a number of social work openings in Waseca and nearby communities, I decided what I would like to do was to continue working with cancer patients. I asked for an appointment with Harry Linduff, executive of the Minnesota Division of American Cancer Society. I told him that I had heard nothing about American Cancer Society services until three years after my diagnosis. Many patients were not getting their literature. Could I help set up support groups in other Minnesota towns? He said the state division had a similar approach under consideration, an educational program developed by a nurse for her Ph.D. study. He showed me her outline for classes called "Living with Cancer." It looked great! He suggested I call the nurse, Judi Johnson.

I sensed her surprise when Judi exclaimed, "You're a patient? Can you come to North Memorial Medical Center in Minneapolis? I am presenting the program to the hospital staff an hour from now. You can come, too, if you would." I had phoned while we were already in Minneapolis, where Bill was attending a legal meeting. So, in less than an hour I was at North Memorial Medical Center. There I was to find many new relationships and opportunities that were to expand and focus the direction of my life.

Judi Johnson and her nurse friend, Pat Norby, had developed a series of eight classes to better inform cancer patients about their disease. For her doctoral research, Judi used several tests to evaluate the program's effectiveness. Results showed that through the combination of class content and interaction with other patients and staff, patients not only gained more accurate information about their disease, but they also experienced less fear and anxiety—*and* a better sense of self worth.

For several weeks I returned to Minneapolis to attend the classes. Representatives of American Cancer Society and a media team were there to evaluate whether and how the model could be "packaged" as an American Cancer Society program. I returned home fired up with enthusiasm. In great detail, I planned how we could offer a similar program at our Waseca Area Memorial Hospital, a progressive 35-bed hospital with dedicated staff. Resource people and speakers were readily available from the Waseca branch of the University of Minnesota. Judi and Pat's outline and objectives for each class served as my guidelines. Now our Make

Today Count group had a great project! Our participants, both professionals and patients, were eager and
committed. It was tremendously successful.

Look for new windows and doors opening

Members of the media team working with American Cancer Society called me several times for suggestions on adjustments and changes that could make the
program useful to small as well as large hospitals. The
program was renamed "I Can Cope." When it was
presented to all Minnesota hospitals, I was thrilled to be
part of the volunteer staff for those presentations. New
friendships, new working relationships, new doors were
opening wide. I became acquainted with nurses and
hospitals all over the state. That was especially reassuring when I was hospitalized for emergency care in
other towns and found friends working there.

I was asked by the American Cancer Society to
chair the statewide advisory committee for I Can Cope.
Through those experiences and relationships, I learned
a lot more about cancer care and treatment. I talked
with hospital social workers, nurses, chaplains and doctors about implementing the program. It was the nurses
who usually had the enthusiasm and the skill to make
the program viable.

The American Cancer Society's national administration had assumed the program was designed only
for the largest treatment centers.

Judi said, "Oh no, it works in small hospitals too."

"Well, perhaps in hospitals over 300 beds."

"No," said Judi, "small hospitals."

"Certainly not those with less 100 beds."

"It works at a 35-bed hospital in Waseca, Minnesota!" said Judi.

I shared in Judi and Pat's satisfaction when American Cancer Society decided to promote it as a national

program for all hospitals. (For more information about I Can Cope, consult your state's American Cancer Society and read the book *I Can Cope*[1] by Judi Johnson and Linda Klein.)

Sometimes I wished I had been the one to develop an educational program, but I realized I had neither the training nor the contacts to do the extensive work Judi and Pat did. I recalled a saying that "Candles give off light, but a mirror reflecting that light can reach farther than the candle by itself." I was content to be a mirror.

Over and over, I wondered and marveled at God's purposeful ways and interventions. I had discovered a place to work, a reason to be.

The American Cancer Society welcomed my volunteered services. Their activities' wide-ranging scope makes room for whatever help one can give in time, in funds or in service. American Cancer Society's Minnesota division is distinctive in its utilization of volunteers. A small core staff keeps the office going, keeps records and coordinates activities. But thousands of volunteers across Minnesota meet the challenge of raising funds and providing valuable services. Cooperation between staff and volunteers has been excellent.

To learn more, I attended many conferences and workshops offered by hospitals, nursing homes and American Cancer Society. I accepted the offer to be professional education chairman in Waseca County. When the Minnesota Coalition for Terminal Care contacted me to arrange a conference for health professionals in our area, I met another group of dedicated people with challenging ideas.

When I heard speakers whose knowledge I felt was pertinent, I invited them for our next professional education conference in Waseca. It was a thrill for me to exchange ideas and experiences with others and to find threads that united us in a common cause. My new goal was to see a hospice program develop in Waseca.

My training as a social worker gave me doubts at first about sick people helping sick people, or worse yet, people without adequate training doing a great deal of harm. Yet my previous experiences in Al-Anon led me to recognize that there is tremendous power in people with similar circumstances meeting together. I saw miracles happen time and again in Alcoholics Anonymous and Al-Anon. The struggles to achieve serenity were very similar, no matter what the disease.

As our Make Today Count group continued to meet month after month, I often wished for another Al-Anon member to become a part of the group because Al-Anon members knew how to interact as a group. They had the right tools to change a discussion from self-pity to progress. One of the things our Make Today Count group did not have was a set of guidelines, sort of like the 12 Boy Scout Laws, or the 12 steps and 12 traditions of Alcoholics Anonymous. I developed my own set of guidelines to achieving serenity with my cancer.

Summary of
My 10 Steps or Guidelines—

1. Recognize my disease and accept help.

2. Learn all I can about my disease.

3. Realize I still have choices.

4. Pray with gratitude for guidance.

5. Put myself in motion.

6. Do everything with gratitude.

7. Believe in God.

8. Accept challenges.

9. Accept weakness and limitations.

10. Give praise.

Strategies for Coping

I will—

1. Recognize that I have a disease and will need the help of God, medical personnel and friends to continue my life.
2. Learn all I can about my disease, realizing that fear can impede my progress more than any known fact.
3. Realize that I still have choices. The disease continues, but I can choose *how* to live with it.
4. Start each day with a prayer of gratitude to God for giving me this day and ask for His guidance in how I use it.
5. Put myself in motion doing whatever task is given me to do, whether it is staying in bed and accepting treatment, or performing a minimal act such as giving care to a plant or a pet.
6. Whatever I do, do it with gratitude, not with a complaint, not looking for pity, not looking for praise—just gratitude that I have life.
7. Believe that I need the help of God and my fellow man to live with my illness, and that through suffering I, and others, can be brought nearer to God.
8. Realize that I am especially challenged if I have a physical illness, for through such weakness the strength and power of our Lord becomes more visible.
9. Accept the weakness given to me. Asking and receiving God's help can give me peace that passes understanding.
10. Realize that praise and gratitude for wherever I am, and whatever I am, is the key to feeling right with myself, my fellow man and right with God."

New Goals for Life

Illness changed my way of life. It made me eliminate some of my previous activities; but it did not eliminate closeness to God nor to activities in which He wanted me to participate. In fact the very same illness made me more aware of God and what He wanted me to do. I had the choice: I could be cheerful—or complaining with my illness. I could be smiling—or moaning with pain. I could do what I could and do it with joy—or lament those things that were past and that I could no longer do.

I prayed, not for healing and self comfort from the agony of disease, but rather for God's guidance. I prayed that sick or well, I would be patient and understand what He wanted me to do. God's grace would give me the strength to endure, the wisdom to see His will for me, the courage to speak and do and live for Him, regardless of the physical ills of my body, or the ills of the world around me.

I have been impressed by the resolve and courage of patients who find positives, rather than create a battle against the negatives. Although thinking about "fighting" and "beating this thing" may show determination, such thoughts also create tension and may build walls of immutability. Instead, the need is to tear down walls of despair and fear. Family members usually are not as much help as fellow patients. Family members are too caught in shock and fear themselves and often feel like helpless bystanders. Family members and patient try to protect each other. Patients can and do adjust more quickly because they are "in the action." There is a black-out period, likened to an astronaut's flight, when at the most crucial times communication may be shut off. The very best thing both patient and family can do is to be open about feelings and worries. Sharing thoughts, even tears, can build bonds of closeness.

At a retreat I attended, I wrote the following purpose for life:

"It seems that God has put two purposes in life: One is to enjoy His gifts of beauty, nature, friendship, love, family and the wonderful, magnificent systems of micro and macrocosm.

"The other is to give service, help and comfort to anything struggling or hurting within my reach.

"If I fail to see and do in either area, life becomes unmanageable. To experience both, in as much fullness as possible, gives meaning, excitement, happiness and serenity to life." How difficult it was to not let cancer get in the way. Any pain occurring and persisting made me wonder if it was another sign of malignancy.

> *I knew I had two choices each morning: Count my aches and feel miserable, or give them to God and medical science. That was their business, and I'd go about mine.*

Reaching Out

The question arose frequently: How soon and in what way should our Make Today Count group reach out to new patients? Bill reminded me how alone I felt fighting cancer those first three years. Usually patients do not know whom to call or what help is available. Therefore, my policy was to make an initial contact with each new patient, hold out a hand and leave the response up to the patient. Some were eager and immediately joined our group for support. Others wanted no part of such a fellowship. Still others declined at first but joined later when their circumstances changed. My experience with Sally was unforgettable and taught me a lot.

Sally was my neighbor. Although she lived a block away, we rarely saw each other. I knew she had had cancer several years ago. Her husband was putting up wallpaper in Bill's new study. I talked with him about asking Sally to join our Make Today Count group. Her husband said he didn't think so. She was back to work and didn't like to talk about cancer.

Two years passed. One day Sally's husband called me on the phone and told me Sally's cancer had returned.

"I think we need to talk," he said, "Can you come over?" It did not take me long to walk the block to their house. Sally's two sisters were there also, along with the three children, ages 9, 11 and 13. I explained about the Make Today Count group and about the I Can Cope classes for patients and family members. Her husband said "I'll call tomorrow and sign up."

"No," said Sally, insistently, "Call right now. I want to be sure we go." Before the first class convened, Sally was hospitalized. Her medical condition indicated that she might not recover. She was too ill to come to I Can Cope class, so we took turns visiting her. On one particular night her two sisters sat in the corner of the room crying quietly. Her husband stood beside her in an effort to console her. As I sat down on the corner of her bed, I was a bit surprised by Sally's opening words to me:

"What bothers me the most is no longer being able to be a good mother for my children."

"Sally, tell me about some of the things you and the children did when you were home with them," I said. "What gave you satisfaction and pleasure and made you feel like a good mother?"

I hoped the question would trigger some happy memories.

"One of the best times was when they came home from school. I'd watch them cross the railroad track, give them a hug when they came in, and then we'd look at their school papers. But those days are gone, I can't do that any more."

"Oh Sally, those children will be coming in the hospital door in a short time. You don't have cancer in your arm—you can still greet them with a hug. You don't have cancer in your smile muscles either. You can still smile and make them feel good."

I paused—almost stunned by what I'd said. It came out so quickly. Did I go too far? Was I too blunt?

There was a momentary silence. Then Sally turned her head, looked at her husband, and gave him a warm loving smile. I could feel the atmosphere in the room change. The dismal despair was changed to caring warmth. I felt it. Did they?

Every day thereafter when I visited Sally, she proudly told me, "I smiled at someone today." She lived for three more weeks.

I am certain her family's final memories of Sally are more blessed because she made them feel love with her hugs and her smiles. The sorting out of what she still could do required the help of a fellow patient. The courage and the will to do all she could came from within Sally.

My Commission

A Make Today Count group in St. Cloud, Minnesota, asked me to participate on a panel with other patients. On the way home, I was rehashing what I had said. Compared with some of the other speakers, I was sure I had fallen short. With that feeling uppermost, it seemed that giving talks in other towns was not as rewarding as working with patients and friends at home. With continuity of contact, it was much easier to tell what was helpful.

Another time I was driving home from Lake City where I had spoken to the nursing staff. While replaying the presentation in my mind and second guessing the words spoken, I tuned the radio to a classical music station. As the music reached its climax, the sky became glowing bright. Rays of light arose from a focal point on the horizon. It was so awe inspiring I pulled over and stopped the car. As I looked at the sky and listened to the stirring music I heard,

"Why are you worrying about your meager words. Don't you know that the power and the glory of the world are Mine. Just keep going down the road you're on."

It was unmistakable and very real. My feeling was humility, surprise and awe. I was certain that I had been given direction by God. As I started the car and continued my journey home, I looked again at the sky. The night was clear, the stars were bright; there was no hint of the phenomenon I had witnessed.

When I got home I told Bill about it. He believed me because direct words from God had changed his life, not many years before, when he was in Hazelden Center for alcoholic treatment. Now a commission had been given for my life to talk and to be with other patients. Whenever I was asked to talk, I talked. When I was asked to visit, I visited.

In the morning when I prayed for help with the day, I no longer asked God to help me. I asked God to let me help Him. He was guiding. I did not have to worry; just follow Him down the road I was on.

MY PRAYER

As my physical body struggles with this disease, help me to feel Thy love for me, O God, shown through the loving hands of the people caring for my sick body.

Help me to bear discomforts strongly and with unending faith.

Help me to receive, with praise and gratitude on my lips.

Help me to see doors of experience and wisdom opening to me, that I may know where you'd have me go and how you'd have me serve.

Take up my fear and replace it with quiet confidence.

Take up my doubts, my frowns, my complaints,

Replace them with smiles, loving touches and gratitude.

And help me to live so that even through my illness, others may see the wonder of Thy loving care.

Amen.

*Take responsibility for yourself
and your needs.*

Thank you, Lord, for each new day.

*Live, learn and do all you can.
Do more than is expected.*

5

Traumatic Side Effects

In the fall of 1977, Patti was in her last year of college. She invited us to Homecoming to meet a young man from California whom she had met at a church conference. He wanted to marry her. The night before we were to leave, I had severe abdominal pains, so severe that we called the doctor. He made a house call and gave me a shot of Demerol and sparine. A short time later, I vomited profusely and had a convulsive seizure. The next day I was "washed out" but the pain was gone. We packed up our suitcases and left. The previous night's experience had left me feeling weak and dehydrated, but it didn't dampen our enthusiasm. We went to the football game and yelled, enjoyed the Norske dinner and danced to Big Band music. Most important, we liked the bearded young man who wanted to marry our daughter. I was absolutely certain that last night's episode was not triggered by anxiety, but it left me puzzled.

A trip to Mexico

During subsequent months, those particular spasms of pain kept recurring. On an extensive trip to Mexico, I had a severe and long-lasting attack. On the way, I became ill while we were in Oklahoma, so we checked into a motel. We didn't know anything about the medical care there, and Bill was very reluctant to take me to a physician who didn't know my history. I became sicker, vomited profusely and passed out. Bill revived me with mouth-to-mouth resuscitation; then he had to clean up the carpet, my slippers, my sweater and me.

Pains continued to occur off and on for several days. I didn't eat very much as we entered Mexico. I learned how to say "sopa and bolillos"—soup and those very good Mexican rolls. On the first night in a Mexican motel, the pains intensified. I prayed fervently for God to help me through the night. I felt I must see a doctor when we got to Mexico City. How in the world would I find one? My first thought was to call the Girl Scout office because Waseca Girl Scouts had gone to the Cabana in Cuernavaca. There must be an English-speaking doctor available. A name and number were given to me and I placed the call. The doctor's wife answered and said I could not see him because he was at the hospital—not seeing patients, but as a patient himself.

The next day we toured the pyramids and met a pediatric surgeon from New Jersey. He was there for a medical convention and he promised to get information about whom I might see. He gave me some children's medicine to help relieve the pain. The following day he called with the name and phone number of a Mexican doctor who spoke English. When I called him, a Spanish-speaking secretary answered and could not understand me. She put the doctor on the line. Yes, he would see me about 7:30 that evening, if we could find his office on Passeo De La Reforma. I was sure we would have no trouble, since that was the main thoroughfare. We were surprised that he kept office hours so late in the evening. Only later did we understand that it was the custom for everyone to close down for an afternoon siesta and stay open in the evening.

We drove downtown to the right address but could see no doctor's office and no parking place. Bill let me off to find the office while he parked the car. I could not find the office nor anyone who understood English, even in the heart of Mexico City. I continued asking for "un medico" and a man motioned me to follow him. Could I trust him? He took me up in an elevator and pointed down the hall. I opened the door. It was a bank. I asked for "telefono" to call the doctor again. He was *not* downtown but at the outskirts of town where the address numbers were repeated in a second series. He had several other appointments. He said he would be in the office late and would wait for me.

We got lost more than once, and it was almost 10 o'clock. What a relief to find that the doctor was still waiting. I was reassured to learn that he was trained at M.D. Anderson Hospital in Houston, Texas. However, he too was a pediatrician. He took my history, examined me and gave me two prescriptions. We learned more about Mexican medical care the next day when we tried to get the prescriptions filled. There were pharmacies, but no pharmacists. Pharmacies did not have the medicines prescribed, as we searched from town to town on our way to our destination at Valle De Bravo. Finally, a stock boy looked in the shelves of medicine until he found what was written on the prescription. He gave it to me with no directions as to how the medicine was to be taken.

The whole experience was very disconcerting. We decided right then that we would confine our travels to the continental United States. Our projected trip to the Holy Land and plans for trips to Europe and Scandinavia would not materialize.

Bowel obstructions

When we returned home, I consulted my oncologist, but he had no explanation for my problem. I consulted the radiation therapist, who had been understanding and helpful before. He told me that my small intestines were "locked down" by adhesions. Radiation treatment sometimes did that. He described my intestine as resembling an old hose that had been left out in the sun for 100 years. It was no longer flexible but was sticky, stiff and scarred. When food, liquid or gas bubbles got stuck in one of the loops, they did not move and caused a small bowel obstruction. When that happened, he said I should go to the hospital for emergency treatment. A build up of toxins from an unresolved obstruction might cause death.

Over ensuing years, the episodes of small bowel obstruction became increasingly frequent, averaging about once a week. At first I tried to "tough it out" as long as possible. I learned that it was much better to get emergency care in the early stages of obstruction, before the painful spasms were so severe that I passed out. Hospital emergency rooms became quite familiar to us. When the nurses and doctors at our Waseca Hospital heard Bill's voice say, "I'm bringing Marvyl in," they would prepare the necessary medication before I was even at the door. I carried a letter from my doctor to give to medical personnel when I needed care out of town. When traveling, we would locate the hospital before deciding on our motel. Many times we made that emergency run, and it became an automatic part of our travel strategy.

I might be cleaning the house or playing on the golf course, happy and relaxed, when the painful spasms began. Doctors said there were no preventative measures. Surgery would not correct the problem but would make it worse by causing more adhesions to form. There was not enough healthy bowel tissue to cut out the bad and repair it. Sutures probably would not hold in irradiated tissue and would not heal because of impaired blood supply and thinned tissues. Also the likelihood of infection was great. The problem could not be corrected.

Sexuality: Coping with changes

Nothing made me so aware of my aching and damaged body as trying to have sexual activity. I could almost forget and ignore my illness, but the realization came crashing down on me when I couldn't respond as a healthy woman. I tried to tolerate the discomfort and pain and override it with my mind, but it was like "the agony and the ecstasy." The ecstasy was so fleeting and I felt depressed with how inadequate I was.

I believe that God gave mankind the pleasures of loving a mate. When illness interfered with the expression of love, it was devastating. During the aggressive phase of treatment, all genital tissues were irradiated because pelvic lymph nodes were malignant. Discomfort was secondary to the importance of aggressive treatment to destroy cancer cells. During nine days of radiation it became progressively worse. During three weeks of "rest," it became an agonizing problem. As if I had sat upon a campfire, all the skin of the upper thighs and labia was black and oozing. It itched terribly and I used some special lotion concocted by clinic pharmacists. As it healed the tissues became thickened and wrinkled. By the time it improved a little with sitz baths and the lotion, it was time for another treatment and a repeat of the agony. Each course of treatment in 1973 and 1975 had its effects of nausea, diarrhea, fatigue, weight loss and sexual changes, but nobody totally assessed the damage.

When it was all over, I slowly regained strength, appetite and energy, but no desire for sexual contact. No desire? Worse than that: aversion and pain with any touch on genital tissue! Even the touch of clothing was irritating. In spite of the lost weight, slacks were binding in the crotch. I was uncomfortable from dryness when walking or sitting. I was uncomfortable most of the time, but not in an area I could talk about. It was hard to discuss such intimate questions with anyone, doctor or spouse. I did not want to hurt my husband's feelings by telling him I had no desire.

I asked for help and was referred to the gynecological section of the clinic. I cannot talk about the insensitivity of some of the doctors without revealing more personal data than I am willing to print. After months of seeing four or five specialists, I was no better. I felt like the proverbial "voice crying in the wilderness." Dear God, who can help me?

Finally, I again returned to my trusted radiation therapist, although contacts with the radiation clinic were supposedly over. He did understand my problem and referred me to a gynecologist who also specialized in cancer care. After an exam, I expected to wait for several days, as usual, to get results. But Dr. Gynecologist himself took the slide to look at it under the microscope. He was back in 10 minutes with the diagnosis that the vaginal tract was full of saprophytic infection, living on the slough of tissue killed by radiation. Also, I was producing no hormones and no lubrication from irradiated glands; tissues were thin and scarred. He prescribed two new medications.

"Local group makes sexuality film"

Our Make Today Count (MTC) members met regularly and talked frankly. I knew I was not the only patient suffering from sexual dysfunction. The subject was alluded to in I Can Cope class, but in a very generic and non-specific way. I approached Dr. Gynecologist to see if he would talk with the I Can Cope (ICC) class.

"What kind of questions do you have?" he asked.

Our ICC class had 40 people in it—patients, health professionals, a mixed group of couples and singles, men and women. Each member of the group wrote questions anonymously. I gave the doctor five pages of questions! He agreed to come to talk with us.

The results were amazing. There was not one single complaint. All were grateful to hear from a doctor who answered their most intimate questions. Dr. Gynecologist commented that the people in the group were so articulate and highly motivated that he felt rewarded, too.

"Great, now how do we get your expertise and knowledge out to all the other I Can Cope classes? Would you write a monograph we could include in the lesson plans?" I asked.

"How about making a videotape of a class in session?" he replied.

"What would you charge us for your time and knowledge and help?" I asked.

"How about a cup of coffee," he answered.

I wrote a script that was checked by the doctor and two nurses from the committee. I contacted the audio-visual staff at the University of Minnesota, Waseca branch, who were eager to cooperate with community projects. They provided us with the studio, the equipment and the technicians free of charge. They charged us only for the materials. Our Make Today Count group had $100 to ante, the American Cancer Society funded $100 and the United Way in Waseca contributed another $100. A number of MTC members were brave enough to be part of the cast in a talk show. Others, who did not want their faces shown, were willing to help in other ways. We rehearsed, we taped, we produced a half hour videotape called, "Sexuality—Coping With Changes Due To Chronic Disease."

One evening when I came home after a meeting, I found my husband laughing at the newspaper. Ordinarily our meeting notices were a small paragraph on the back page. Today the lower quarter of the front page showed a picture of the university photographer and the back of the heads of all video participants, with the headline: "Local Group Makes Sexuality Film." We were suddenly notorious!

The video was shown at the next training session for I Can Cope facilitators and offered for sale at cost. It was reviewed in a national nursing magazine. Orders began to pour in. The university audio-visual shop could not keep up with the demand, so we went to a commercial enterprise. Bookkeeping became a feat that required order blanks and invoice sheets. As the video-tape became known, we were thrilled to send it out from Waseca Memorial Hospital to nursing schools and cancer centers all over the United States.

The Wildflower Woodlands

Amidst the threats and the fears prompted by my illness, I had many life-affirming activities. I recalled a song that was sung by one hundred little girls to open day camp in Maplewood Park.

> "God has created a new day
> Silver and green and gold
> Live that the sunset may find you
> Worthy His gifts to hold."

From The Ditty Bag by Janet E. Tobitt
Girl Scouts of America, Used by permission.

God's world of nature and God's world of people had been important to me since childhood. I was a Girl Scout, a camp counselor, then a leader, and worked in the scout office for a time. I directed day camp at Maplewood Park until cancer treatment interfered. I worked with the Waseca County Extension Service to teach bird identification to the fifth and sixth grade classes from the schools around the county. I served as a guide for nature hikes for children and adults.

In the spring of 1980, the University of Minnesota School of Agriculture in Waseca offered a class in wild flower identification in the Horticulture Department. I was invited to be a consultant for a year, and then the next four years I was asked to teach the course. It was stimulating, refreshing and wonderful to go out in the woodlands twice a week. Certainly God was giving me opportunities to replenish my health.

It was not without its challenges though, for the wildflower woodlands we explored were without restrooms. It was there that I realized the magnitude of my problems. The aftermath of the small bowel obstructions, which continued to occur, was an uncontrollable, odiferous and profuse dumping of bowel contents a few days after each obstruction. With no restrooms in sight, I had an embarrassing accident in the woods with students around me. My next exploration was to the drug store, to look for adult diapers.

National coverage

Teaching at the university, teaching I Can Cope classes at the hospital and to nurses throughout the state, as well as an occasional class at area technical colleges, speaking at American Cancer Society workshops and at many churches, service clubs and nursing homes in Southern Minnesota helped me feel very fulfilled and useful.

A person from the national office of the American Cancer Society called one day to ask about taking pictures of an I Can Cope class in session. They wanted pictures from rural Minnesota with "lots of local color." It was a cold blustery November day when two photographers arrived from New York City. I don't know what they expected, but they were surprised at the beauty of Minnesota, even on a gray, bleak November day! They spent two days taking hundreds of pictures in our hospital, of the farms and of people who came to I Can Cope classes. A month or so later I was in the Minneapolis Cancer Society office, just after the mail had arrived. On every desk was a copy of the national magazine *Cancer News* with a full cover picture of me hugging a fellow patient from I Can Cope class. Inside the magazine were more pictures to accompany the news story. Some of the other photographs taken appeared on national posters and pamphlets, surprising me each time.

God was indeed giving me new days, new opportunities, new ways to serve Him.

I thought of the time when Nancy and I were co-chairmen for the programs of Ladies Friendly Group 3 at our Congregational church. When we studied the parables, we had discussed whether we earned our way to salvation. My mother used to say good deeds put stars in our crowns. My thoughts were changed by our group's discussions; good deeds are *not* for climbing a ladder to God's grace. First we believe; then the results are a desire to do good. The Bible is not just old history. New insights came flooding in. Studying those phrases is helpful today.

Our study guide quoted from Paul's first letter to the Thessalonians: "Rejoice evermore. Pray without ceasing. In everything give thanks; for this is the will of God in Christ Jesus concerning you." [5:16-18 NIV]

But could I say thanks for my cancer? For the years of pain? For Bill's alcoholic disease? Did I have enough faith to say thanks for things that hurt me?

I remember now how surprised I was when I tried it. I was walking down the gravel road by the golf course, upset by a misunderstanding with my husband. With exasperation and doubt I said, "Thank you God for the problem Bill and I have right now. Help me to learn from it." As soon as the words were out of my mouth, another point of view popped into my head. It worked!

I recalled another time when I was angry at the doctor and at my husband for giving me orders and bossing me around. It seemed they didn't care how I felt. I picked up my Bible and walked out on the deck, away from everybody. I flipped through the pages looking for something useful. The words leaped out from the page. "I have given you strong arms to support you in your weakness." Gratitude replaced my anger.

I remembered how during the pain of small bowel obstruction, instead of praying for relief from pain I began to pray for endurance and strength. I prayed for learning and understanding for myself or my doctors. I prayed "Help me to hear you, O God, to feel your presence." Paul said to the Romans [5:3-5 NIV] that we can "rejoice in our sufferings, knowing that suffering produces endurance, endurance produces character, character produces patience and hope, and hope does not disappoint us."

Boy! Did I learn endurance! . . . And patience . . . And hope!

Without suffering, without problems, I would have no need to turn to God for help and no need to turn to others for help. Pain problems taught me to endure and be strengthened. If I had no more pain nor problems with my cancer, how could I understand the persistent pain and problems of others? Couldn't I be more helpful now to other patients?

It seemed entirely backwards and incongruous to say thanks for a problem. It took blind courage and faith to do so. The answer I received was always an unexpected way of seeing and understanding that I did not have before. Fr. John Powell gave criteria for knowing when God speaks to us. Powell said:

> *"There is always an element of surprise.*
> *There is an element of certainty,*
> *There is an ability to be changed by the experience."*
> *He Touched Me*[2] by Fr. John Powell (Quoted by Permission)

Since we lived on a hill right next to the golf course, I attended some of the ladies' country club meetings. I felt impatient with some of the petty grumblings and disagreements. Time was "awasting" while we argued over the color of the restroom wallpaper. Time was something I might not have much of. I didn't want to spend it arguing. I was not having fun there. Like my earlier experience at our legislator's picnic, I felt like a "drop in" from another world.

Why did I feel better spending time with cancer patients than "playing." Was something wrong with me that I got satisfaction and hope out of visiting the ill? I thought of Christ's words, that he came not to be with the well, but to heal the sick. We were to follow His example: "Whoever wants to become great among you must be your servant." [Matthew 20:26 NIV]

It's all right! I could be more Christ-like. I could serve Him better by continuing to help cancer patients. On a clothesline of troubles, I would never choose cancer as my "cross," nor as my opportunity. But the choice was not mine. I was given it. I have it. Now what could I do with it? God, this was a big one. Help me!

It was my custom each morning to open the bedroom drapes, to check the sky and the weather, and then say "Thank you God for this day, for giving me another day. Help me to get through it. Help me with this task or that responsibility. Help me in this uncertainty or this pain." One morning as I pulled the blue drapes to let the sunlight in, I was shockingly aware that I had it backwards! All these years I had been praying God to help me. My prayer should be, "Let me help You!" What a difference that made! I was no longer in the driver's seat with a multitude of things to do for which I needed help. God was driving! Could I find one small way to help Him this day? Was there something I could do to help someone, or appreciate someone, or to bring a bit more beauty or peace into the world? Lord, help me to discern your special plan.

A dear friend, Fran, who lived with ovarian cancer for eight years, said to me, "You know we're the lucky ones, those of us who have cancer, because we've been forced to take a look at life and set priorities."

Many stories are written by people saying that illness has made them appreciate life more. I felt that way for awhile, but as year after year went on with no surcease of cancer problems, I began to long for those heavenly days. Jesus promised eternal life in God's kingdom of peace and beauty. When would it be my turn? I was truly grateful for the extra years given me, but I was also tired of the struggle. When would I enter His Kingdom?

Backwards me again! This earth, too, is God's kingdom! This earth with all its beauties and mysteries; the joys of friendships and family. O my God, Your kingdom! I am in it now as surely as I will be when I am in heaven. Help me make the most of each day here on this earth.

Set Goals.
Accumulate small successes.

Celebrate small joys.
Look for treasures.

6

Cancer Returns – Chemotherapy

"Everyone should assume responsibility for knowing and understanding his own health care, but often when cancer is involved, fear makes it difficult for people to ask questions or to understand the answers. Our purpose is to inform and to educate and to make this information available to any Minnesotan. Fear subsides when replaced with knowledge." (Quoted by Permission)

I valued those words written in 1977 by Minnesota American Cancer Society President, Dr. Everett Schmitz.

Obviously that opinion was not shared by my doctor. In 1982, nodular masses reoccurred in my armpits and were visible as a large nut-size swelling under my ear. The doctor who coordinated my treatment was placating me and belittling my problems. He patted me on the head or tweaked my nose and told me not to ask so many questions. Small bowel obstructions were occurring 30 to 50 times a year. The doctor refused to acknowledge that difficulty because he had not observed it himself, even though copies of X-rays and notes on emergency treatment had been sent to him from hospitals all over the country—St. Petersburg, Florida; Marquette, Michigan; Chisago Lakes and

Waseca, Minnesota. I requested a referral to a gastroenterologist, but he told me it would do no good. I
asked for biopsy of the lymph nodes. He said the cancer
had recurred and was no longer treatable. I asked for
chemotherapy. He said that with the amount of radiation I had been given, it was not safe to give me chemotherapy. Further treatment would make me sicker without making me better. The plan was to "wait and watch."

That was discouraging!

Take charge

Following a conference, Judi, Pat, Nancy and I
were sitting together sipping cokes at the American
Cancer Society office. We all worked together on the I
Can Cope committee. I told them my dilemma. Their
questions come in rapid succession.

"When are you going for that second opinion?"
"When are you going to take charge? It's your life."
"Are you afraid?"
"Is it the money?"

They bombarded me with questions and direc-
tions. At first I was defensive. I *was* in charge of my life;
I *was* getting the best medical care. I *was* doing good
things to give my life quality. Why were they assailing
me? Then I realized they really heard the questions I
had been asking, which the doctor had ignored or answered with platitudes. They were encouraging me,
not assaulting me. It was almost like an Alcoholic Anonymous confrontation that I had been part of in the past. I
should do something! Take charge and change what I
did not like! It was Second Opinion Time! Judi knew of
a new young woman doctor in Minneapolis who was
doing wonderful things for her patients. I should make
an appointment with her.

Again I sought out my trusted radiation therapist.
He encouraged me to seek a second opinion and would

be glad to cooperate by seeing that my records were transferred.

Dr. Barbara Bowers, the new young oncologist at North Memorial Medical Center in Minneapolis, listened carefully to everything Bill and I had to say. Her examining technique was extremely gentle compared with the male doctors I had previously had. She was thorough and thoughtful. All of the previous tests and biopsies were redone for evaluation of current status. Yes, the cancer was growing again—poorly differentiated nodular lymphoma that had spread throughout the body. She consulted with tumor boards of three Minneapolis hospitals. The Rochester Mayo Clinic approach was a valid one, but on the other hand, I was a virgin as far as chemotherapy was concerned. It was worth giving it a try to see if my body could tolerate it. She was concerned and creative.

"First, let's try to prevent the small bowel obstructions by breaking up the normal gas bubbles into smaller ones that can pass through, and thus prevent the obstructions from occurring." With a simple medication, the incidence of obstructions was cut in half over the next few months!

"Let's start a dose of chemotherapy with only a single agent," she said. My new doctor monitored not only my blood counts but the way I was feeling, the amount of nausea I had; she adjusted the dose accordingly. The first couple of weeks I was nauseated and woozy, but as time went by and adjustments were made, it became relatively easy to take a chemotherapy drug by mouth every day. Within a very short time, the swelling of the malignant neck nodes went down.

During that time of chemotherapy, the good results were not always apparent, however. Recurrence of cancer for the third time, and its subsequent treatment led to some times of discouragement.

Writing in my journal helped a lot. I wrote:

*I am really down this month. I am discouraged, I hurt, I
feel inadequate, criticized, not worthwhile. I don't like to be
this way. I don't like myself this way. I'm hard to live with
when I'm this way. I feel anger, resentment and self-pity. I
can justify those feelings, I have a right to them. But I know I
must rid myself of the poisons of indignation, resentment and
self-pity if I am to find serenity and happiness again. I want
to feel happy again. Yet, day after day I wake up mad. I live
through the day trying to hide the bitterness and discouragement I feel. How can I get rid of it?*

Long ago I began putting thoughts down in a journal when I felt I was getting lost in the cracks of medical
care. Clinic specialists saw me every month or two.
Local doctors took care of needs in between. Emergency room doctors in many hospitals took care of me
while we were traveling. Nobody saw the "whole me"
and nobody put the pieces together. To accurately relate the sequence of events, I began to keep my own
record, keeping track of tests and also writing down my
feelings. I lived with repeated episodes of pain, discomfort and embarrassment. In these days of modern medicine, cancer is often a prolonged affair. It doesn't always kill quickly. I may not even die from it, but the
living sure isn't easy.

One day, I made two columns to write my feelings.
I started with the bad times. Then I paired these with a
positive counterpoint—and I titled it "How many times
this month did I feel (Bad) and how many times did I
feel (Good).

HOW MANY TIMES THIS MONTH DID I FEEL

(BAD)

Have to ingest poison to
control cancer cells.......... 14
Feel nauseated 7
Vomit............................ 2
Intense pain of obstruction ... 11
Need morphine or belladonna 5
Bladder or bowel accidents.... 7
Go to bed with tears from pain 5
Have a liquid diet 14
Have restless night............. 2
Feel criticism from others... few
Feel self-criticism .... many

(GOOD)

Remember chemo is effective??
Walk outdoors............... 12
Admitted to hospital........ 1
Have no BM problems...... 20
Wear diapers.................. 14
Make it to the bathroom ... 45
Get help from MD, RN, PHM. 3
Eat normal meal............. 68
Good nights sleep 28
Spend time with friends ... 12
Hear "I love you"......over 100
See my children ...... over 50
Get out for fun 3
Sing 8
Attend meetings 10
Read for inspiration......... 36

The bad times had seemed so all consuming. It was helpful to total up the good times and to realize they were greater than the bad times. It took determination to focus on the positive and to realize that was My responsibility. I reflected on the five stages of loss as frequently cited from the Kubler-Ross books: Denial — Anger — Despair — Bargaining — and Acceptance. It is important to add a sixth stage: *Responsibility*. I have to take responsibility for my emotions and resulting actions.

Often other people came to Make Today Count meetings with discouragement showing in their faces, too. There was nothing wrong with being "down." It's a natural reaction to bad news. But I did not like being there. If I didn't want to stay down, I had to devise some steps to get me up.

Guidelines for getting
'up' from the 'downs'

1. PRAY—for patience, for learning, not for removal of the problem, but for help in bearing it. When I get up, open the bedroom curtains, look up and say "Good Morning God, be with me today." Say it out loud, as a child would coming in from school and saying, "Hi Mom, I'm home."

2. READ—Sit long enough to read the Bible, some inspirational literature, devotions, poetry, someone else's inspiring words. Think about what I'm reading. Put some positive thoughts into that computer brain that is spitting out negatives.

3. EXERCISE—Use some big muscles, breathe deeply, get outdoors, do some physical activity.

4. BE—with other people—interact, laugh, listen, help, receive.

5. DO—something, anything: water a plant, pet a pet, dust a table, get my own drink, write a note—succeed in doing at least **one** thing each day.

6. WRITE—put down on paper my thoughts, my feelings, my frustrations, my goals. Maybe I'll share with others what I've written, maybe not.

7. WAIT—Allow time to heal, time to adjust.

8. WANT TO—want to give up my self-pity, to let go of the anger—want to do it enough to change.

At the end of a year, a CT scan showed that the swollen malignant lymph nodes had shrunk in size. We tried another year of chemotherapy. There was more reduction in node size. At the end of the third year the nodes were almost normal. After three years of chemotherapy, I was in remission! Controlled disease was far different from cured disease, though, and I would need close monitoring for all of my life. With Stage 3 lymphoma there are no cures; sooner or later it always recurs.

But my life was prolonged! I was given the precious gift of being able to welcome into this world another generation—our grandchildren.

Our first grandchild, Mara Lynn, was born in 1981 on our wedding anniversary. We rushed to the hospital in Minneapolis and were welcomed by her parents, Paul and Lynn. The nurses brought us white gowns, masks, a rocking chair and the precious blanket-wrapped baby. How different from 31 years ago when our Paul was born. Then grandparents could view only through the nursery window. We reflected awe and wonder at this anniversary gift. We rocked her, we unwrapped her, we counted each toe. We loved her with that quick flow of absolute love that is God's gift to grandparents.

A few weeks later we planned to go to California to help usher in our second grandchild, whose mother is our daughter. However, one of those troublesome blood clots formed in my leg, and the doctor recommended waiting a bit before taking a long flight. Hot packs and elevation helped the clot dissolve and I prepared to travel. Another clot formed. Another week of bed rest. Up again. Another clot. Back to bed rest. More hot packs, more elevation of my right leg. Discouragement. Baby Christopher was born and I was not there. More blood clots kept forming. Would I ever get to see him? I could scarcely imagine our Patti pregnant, and now the baby was born. I was trying to be patient, but oh, how I wanted to be in California!

A Community Service Award

One day, Bill began to get out our good dishes. He told me we were to have company that evening after the awards dinner, where his law partner was receiving an honor. He wanted to invite a few people to celebrate. I was not to get up to help; the other wives would bring the snack food and drinks. The doctor told him I could get up to shower and go to the award ceremony, if I was careful and wore support stockings. I called the drugstore to fill my prescription for a new pair of heavy rubber hose. I put the hose on. When I stood up, they slid down to my knees. I called the pharmacist to ask how I was to hold them up, what did the company provide? Nothing. Neither the druggist, the department store, nor the dime store had anything like a garter belt or girdle at that time, when panty hose were new. A neighbor brought over a XXX large girdle. When I put it on, it fell to my knees along with the hose.

I got in the shower and cried. I wanted to be *up*. I wanted to go to California! I wanted to go to the ceremony. I couldn't find anything to hold up those stupid stockings. Finally, I dug out some old garters and a panty girdle from way back in the drawer. I snapped eight garters together on the panty girdle, and hoped. I shampooed and set my hair with curlers. I put on my best wine-colored velveteen dress with the black trim. I was not very secure about being ready to celebrate the evening.

After a nice dinner at the Eagles Club, the Master of Ceremonies began his spiel. The recipient of this Community Service award was always kept a secret until the last minute. I expected Bill's partner would be surprised; but then I heard my name called. The entire roomful of people rose to their feet. I was overwhelmed!

Tears came to my eyes as I walked to the platform. After the applause died down, I responded by telling about my despair that afternoon, how I cried in the shower. I told them that I'd found the way to create a meaningful life was to serve and give without counting. I thanked them for the honor that had come so unexpectedly.

I saw our son Paul go to the platform. He got a big laugh as he unrolled a long sheet of computer paper to read a "short" poem he had written about his mother:

"Tonight we are here to present an award,
To someone we all have good feelings toward.
Every person who knows you agrees you deserve it
Your community thanks you for the ways that you serve it.

There is a custom at these sorts of events
To tell a good story at guest of honor's expense
To those who don't know the whole story, just listen
And corner her later for a small inquisition.

There once was a weekend, we all felt quite lazy,
When suddenly Mom said, "Oh hurry like crazy,
I just now remembered a banquet at eight
Quick put on your good clothes, we mustn't be late."

A chorus of groans, "Do we have to go?
We'd rather just stay home, "but Mom, she said, "NO!"
So we grumbled and hurried, got into the car
And drove to the Ag School. "Well here we are...."

"But this sure is strange, though it's eight on the dot
There's no one else here—not a car in the lot!"
"Oh come on Mom," we said, "check the tickets just once."
"—Let's see—the right time—OOPS, wrong month!"

Mom, you kept us together, made things happy and bright
You helped us through bad times, their impact was slight.
In those times of troubles that we're all subject to,
It was you, more than anyone, who pulled us all through.

Then a few years ago you found out you had cancer.
But withdraw and give up? That wasn't your answer.
With God, friends and family, and the strength that is in you
You found ways to do more than simply continue.

And so strong is the power of these things you believe,
That you found you could give so much more than receive.
You've reached out to others with compassion and caring
And showed them the way to make sickness <u>worth</u> bearing.

In joy and in sorrow you've given your best.
We remember all those good times,
            and we've learned from the rest.
Through thick and through thin, we've cared for each other,
In living, in loving, our teacher was Mother.

                                    (there were 20 verses in all)

To have lived to hear such thanks from children and community, what a tremendous blessing! When we got home, all of my Make Today Count friends were there with food and congratulations. That night my prayers to God were prayers of gratitude for bringing me out of pain to such great joy.

And a week later I went to California to meet baby Chris!

About praying for healing

None of us who are alive get through without some tests of our faith, some pain, some trial, some wall to hurdle, some thorn in our flesh.

Perhaps my understanding about praying for healing is different. It has been done for me many times, and I am grateful for each prayer, each touch, each laying on of hands. But I think of Paul's word to the Corinthians, Through my weakness the strength of God is more visible. (II Cor. 12:9 my interpretation) Instead of healing, which may not be granted, I would rather prayers are said for my strength to endure, courage and wisdom to see how I should serve Him. If I try to figure out the reasons for all of this, I go around in circles. Instead of saying "why," I do much better if I acknowledge that I have a problem and ask "where to now" and "how." Perhaps my job is not to be set free, but to learn how to live with it. The Son of God was not relieved from pain, neither was Paul or Stephen. Why should I be exempt?

When Bill was struggling with the "why," our former pastor gave him a copy of *The Will of God*[3] by Leslie Weatherhead. It was a great help to him to realize that God's Intentional Will was a happy relationship with man. His Circumstantial Will gave man free will that allows us to make many mistakes. He permits our non-God-like behavior and tragedies to happen. But His Ultimate Will is the accomplishment of God's purpose to redeem man in spite of it all.

Treasure Hunt

"Do other cancer patients sometimes feel like I do? Tired of the endurance contest?

Tired of the changes in body and the constant effort to be whole and well?

Tired of the adaptations made in our thinking and living to accommodate the illness?

I wake up each morning with two opposing thoughts to reconcile:
1. Almost a reluctance to wake up and accept the challenges of another day.
2. Gratitude for the gift of another day and the opportunity it brings for love and for work.

Death has been faced and reconciled so many times these past few years that it holds no terror, only a glorious promise of peace and comfort. And yet, I cannot allow myself to wish for death.

Life itself has been enriched amidst the threats. Each day is like a treasure hunt. What is my treasure today? Perhaps it is the arms of a small child held up to me. Or the warm soft snuggles of a sleepy baby in my arms. Perhaps the unexpected flash of a new bird at the feeder, or the close examination of a blossom with its intricate tiny parts. Perhaps a hug from a friend. Or absorbing every fiber of my husband's embrace.

Sometimes the treasures are laid in my path and all I need to do is pick them up to enjoy. Other days I have to search. Where are my treasures today? I have to look and be aware of the possibilities. Perhaps I need to visit a friend or read a book. Perhaps I'll find it in worship at church or in hearing a song. Perhaps it will be in the listening of a pharmacist, a nurse or a doctor with a helpful answer. Perhaps my treasure will come in a quiet walk where I talk only to my dog and to God— both of whom like to hear my voice.

The wonderful thing is: Always treasures are there. Whether I stumble upon them, or have to look in the dark hidden places, God has placed them there for my joy.

My daughter said to me one day, *'My* life is not God's gift to me. *Your* life is God's gift to me!'

And now, as I think about that, I realize I have things backwards once again.

Instead of struggling to measure up, how calming it is to think that I am God's gift to others, and all those others are God's gift to me! What did Paul say? "Give thanks in all in all circumstances." [I Thess. 5:18 KJV]

"Through my weakness the strength of God is more visible" [II Corinthians 12:9 KJV interpreted]. Help me, God, to live with it. Give me strength to endure, courage to hope, wisdom to see some way in which I may serve Thee.

That is not the same as saying I give up to death or to despair. Rather it is being able to say because of this pain I am more keenly aware of how much I need the help of other human beings, and how much I need the help of God. Lord, give me new vision to find doors of service; open my eyes, my ears, my understanding in new ways. May I learn the lessons and feel less self important now. I need to recognize God's importance—the importance of friends, family and doctors whom I need to help me continue my life. I am not self suffi-cient—I am not indispensable—not almighty. I am a child—I am in need. Once more, I recall the Micah 6:8 verse: "What does the Lord require of you? To act justly, and to love mercy, and to walk humbly with your God."

Each day I choose whether to smile or grumble, whether to complain or to be preoccupied with my own misery. I can lose my life in service, as God wants, and find delight in the blessings.

None of us are so strong that we can do it without help from each other. Reading and talking with others helped me, even re-reading something I wrote awhile ago. But the searching had to be my own. Canned Bible verses to read when weary or distressed were not as effective as searching, putting myself in the posture of seeking and asking. I didn't need to figure it all out. I didn't need to be healed of cancer, I only needed to:

Give thanks. Ask guidance. Trust. Put myself in motion.

Thoughts about dying

I did think about dying, most often when I was not feeling well. Bill and I were present at the death of our parents and each experience taught me something.

Bill's Dad had health problems when they were living in Florida and Bill made several hurried flights to be with him. Finally, it was necessary to bring him home. Bill sold their Florida property at a loss, piled all their belongings in their car and drove back to Minne-sota. I remember the day Dad died. He was at home and fell in the bathroom. Mom called us and the ambulance. We stood by as the attendants carried Dad, uncon-scious, out of the house. His mouth was open and his tongue seemed too big, exactly the way mine felt that very first time I felt the invasion of cancer. He took his last breath as he was carried into the hospital. Afterwards, I sat beside Mom in the hospital lobby, holding her hand as we cried. I remember my hair was in curlers—strange what things one remembers.

Bill's mother was with us four more years. The first sign of trouble appeared when she was helping me prepare Sunday dinner. She tried to peel a coffee cup instead of a potato, and she zipped her dress up and down several times. She had a slight stroke. After that, she was forgetful, but most of the time she was a delightful person. When her colon cancer was diagnosed, she kept her sense of humor, telling us she didn't like the doctor who "cut up her center piece."

As time went on, she lived more in the past. Family members took turns staying with her. What good times we had when we would go back in time with her and learn and laugh about all the pranks she used to play as a young girl on the farm. I was reminded of the words of Russell Baker in his book *Growing Up*.[4] He says the elderly are able to transcend all boundaries of time and space to return to former times when they were whole and capable. I think, perhaps, that is one of God's gifts to elderly people.

On the day of Bill's mother's death, my morning devotional reading happened to fall on I Corinthians 15. In verses 35-44, it tells how we must die and be planted as a seed in the ground to grow wonderful new bodies. Our earthly bodies become weak, old and embarrass us, as did Mom's colostomy.

My own mother's death was unexpected as she died in her sleep. In her later years, Mom had not taken very good care of her personal appearance, but I saw and felt a wonderful sense of her beauty as she lay at peace. For many years, she had talked about a favorite old-time hymn that said death was like a dream. She wanted it sung at her funeral. After her death, my brother's wife and I began to search. A local musician found it in an old hymnal shortly before the service, so we quickly made copies and all of us sang it together.

Before the service, the minister invited my brother and me into his study. He asked us to name the qualities we felt most endearing about Mom. The service was small and informal. Not only did the minister use our words, but he asked friends in the congregation to tell, in a word, what Mom's life had meant to them. It was a blessing beyond anything I could have imagined.

I worried about Dad. For many years he had been deaf, so he had not attended church. After Mom's death, he told me he didn't know what he believed. Many strokes left him with significant weakness and speech that was difficult. One morning before going to the hospital to see him, I read Revelations 3:8. "I know your deeds. See, I have placed before you an open door that no one can shut. I know that you have little strength, yet you have kept my word and have not denied my name."

As I entered the hospital, the chaplain met me and said, "You look like you've just had wonderful news." I had!

The day before death, while Dad was lying in his bed, he suddenly looked up, opened his eyes wide in surprise, then extended his hand and smiled as though greeting a long lost friend. All day long we watched as Dad seemed to meet old friends or family again and again. I said to him, "It's kind of exciting, isn't it Dad?" The next day, as my brother and I held his hand, his noisy breathing became quiet and slow and peaceful. It was a very holy moment when his breath ceased.

Thinking over all these memories, I wrote a few of my thoughts about death.

The flight to heaven—how different it is for each one of us. For some the air is turbulent with many dark clouds. For some the same ascent is smooth and easy. We don't know why it is different, except that each one of us is different and has our own flight pattern. Thinking about Dad today, I feel the stormy weather is over; he is on his way above the clouds. How far he has to climb, I do not know, but he once said to me, "I'll be all right." Whether it takes a week or a month now, his journey has begun. We can go with him part way, we can cheer him on, reassure him of our love and our trust in the goal he seeks.

We regard the moment of birth as miraculous, holy, wonderful—-the transition into the beautiful world, ideally the embodiment of love, trust and faith. Death? Can it not also be a miraculous, holy, wonderful transition? Because of our own feelings of loss, man gives another quality to death. Mystery and the unknown are present in both birth and death. With eyes that are clouded, we deny the beauty and hope that lies in death's transition.

My life, as I live it, and my death, as my relatives and I experience that, can be welcome, holy, and meaningful in all its aspects, if I wholly trust God.

The miracle lies in the ability of Man with God to convert sadness, pain and tragedy, to experience a clearing of eyes and ears, to perceive beauty, hope, meaning. Death is not man's separation from God. Our fear of it is man's separation from God.

"Physical death is not the enemy of the Christian. Have you ever considered what would happen if you couldn't die? The blind would remain blind. The paralyzed would never walk. That which is crooked would remain crooked. Aching hearts would continue to ache. The terminally ill would remain ill, but never terminate. Those who labor for breath would continue in their suffering. For the believer in Jesus Christ, death brings a fresh start, physically, emotionally and spiritually. That new life in Christ, which began on this earth, comes to fullest expression in heaven."

Pastor Jeff Burton, Quoted by permission.

A greater miracle than curing me is God's helping me to live with "it" with joy. If I pray "cure me," the answer I want may not come; if I pray "help me, strengthen my faith, let me feel joy," the answer I want will come.

I ask that God show me what I need to learn or understand through this difficult time. I must patiently wait and keep tuned in, following one step at a time, one moment at a time. As I go up and down this rocky path of living with chronic illness, I sometimes get glimpses and feelings of euphoria. Sometimes I am moved by emotions that bring tears. Sometimes I am in the bottom of the canyon seeking a glimpse of light for guidance and hope. All of these experiences enrich me if I look and listen. Whichever one I am in, I need the hands of others to help me find my way through the valleys and up and down the peaks of experience. Those hands of others—they are part of God's gift to me, and part of my gift to others.

If my physical illness is not going away, if I am to find comfort, I must change how I think. When my faith is strong enough to say "thank you" for this trial today, help me to grow from it, to feel your loving hand. Then I have that peace that "passes understanding."

Thank you God, for this pain, this weakness,
   Which reminds me how much I need you
   And how much I need the help of your people on earth.
I can't take care of me by myself.
Thank you for being there for me to talk to.
Thank you for the comforts of my home, my bed, my hospital,
   And for the people you have put around me to help me.
Thank you for giving me this time to rest and heal.
Help me to learn understanding and compassion for others as
   I stumble along this path of my illness.
Give me vision to see and ears to hear the beauty
   and love you have put around me.
Help me to live showing gratitude.
And to live, that even through my illness, others may see the
   wonder of Thy loving care.
                                        Amen.

Explore new options, new skills.

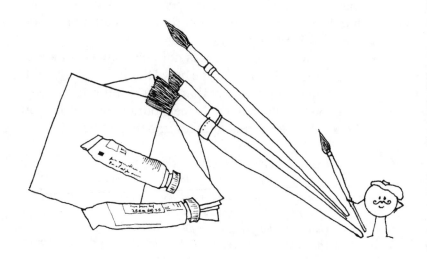

Let the world in.
Let friendships grow.
Seek companionship, not isolation.

7

I'm Going to Live

A deeply slanted section of seats led down to a speaker's podium at St. Olaf College in Northfield, Minnesota. The speaker at this meeting in 1985 was Dr. John Brantner, a distinguished professor from the University of Minnesota School of Medicine, Department of Psychiatry. In any group, he was easily identified by his long gray hair tied into a pony tail with a small black ribbon. His hug, given to the chairman before he began, reflected his warmth. His casual stance, with one foot on a chair, seemed to indicate informality and ease. His voice resonated confidence, his cascading deep laughter revealed a sense of humor.

After warming his audience with true stories that brought gales of laughter, Dr. Brantner turned serious and asked, "Who will survive the onslaughts of something like cancer? Will you? Will I? Besides trusting the medical profession and hoping the treatment is good for me, what can I do to aid in my survival efforts?"

My excitement grew as I jotted down these guidelines for survival.

Keys to surviving

1. Openly *acknowledge* and *express* the negatives you find in your situation and in your feelings. Health depends on learning to be an effective complainer. Be assertive and aggressive, but avoid self-pity. Make light of the problems, but clearly verbalize them. Share the problems to relieve the burdens and to seek answers. Do not tolerate an intolerable situation.

2. *Maintain high morale.* Being sad is normal, being depressed is pathological. Depressed people disengage from life, can't be comforted, can't sleep, can't eat; they are filled with guilt, or remorse or fear. They neglect self care. Every adult has plenty of reasons to feel sad, but celebrate, even in your sadness. Determination can make a difference. Good spirits, high vitality and a sense of humor are important and they are contagious. They can infect others and can be taught to others.

3. *Keep a high level of activity,* physical and mental. Go beyond what is expected. Take energy from others and release it in other forms. Learn something new, do something you've always wanted to do. Also be skilled at *relaxation.* Practice relaxation until you can do it to Olympic proportions. Enjoy well used solitude.

4. *Be sociable.* Seek out casual encounters. Deliberately build social and group support. Join a support group. Repeatedly seek and receive new information. Become a network member to gain love, value and esteem.

5. *Be diverse.* Seek and enjoy companionship of all ages. Deliberately reach out. Constantly be replenished

by new experiences and contacts. Enjoy the rich glory of differences. Learn to be attractive, even be flamboyant, be noticed.

6. *Follow a spiritual path.* Develop a firm under girding. Be active spiritually, which provides an interior peace. Make catastrophe a positive force. Make a challenge of the difficulties. Know you have value. Develop self-esteem.

7. *Assume responsibility* for meeting your own needs. Find out what the choices are and make decisions. Simplify your goals, but do something each day. Accumulate successes.

8. *Take encouragement.* Enjoy singing and music, not silence. Let the world intrude upon you. Narrowing your space and your interests leads to despair. There should be constant morale-building activities. Show expressions of delight as well as sadness.

Did he say seek new experiences, be noticed, be flamboyant? It is not what sick people usually do. We tend to want to hide and cover up our imperfect-ness. All day long I had been feeling self-conscious about intruding on the speaker by periodically going to the stage to change the tapes recording his message. As I realized what he had said, I was not only happy I had had that job, but I was glad I had worn a conspicuously bright red suit! When the day was over I felt that I could put exclamations marks all over the place. That's the way that I am living with cancer! I dashed home and told my husband excitedly, "I'm going to live!!!"

My journal for the next few weeks shows my efforts to process all this new information.

April 1985

I need the best medical help I can get, but I also need to look at what is subject to my control. Diet, exercise and rest are important and so is what I 'breathe in' important. Things I touch and reach for are important, so are my thoughts and my readings. If life is shorter than I expected, that is of lesser importance than full, rich, productive quality of my survival time.

*Strangely, when I read stories of miraculous healing, I do not seek a miraculous healing. It is more of a miracle that I am living and living **well** with my disease. If God took away my cancer, the service I'm learning to give would no longer be possible. The appreciation and understanding of His love would not be so visible.*

I reread thoughts of writers who seem to have a glimpse of God's power. When I think about the people I know who have serious troubles, some are devastated; others not only surmount the problems but seem to radiate joy and gratefulness. Do any of the people who radiate joy and gratitude say they did it by themselves? The ones I know give credit to God who helped them.

There are days when I know and feel God's warmth and direction near me. There are other days when I wonder if I imagine it. Is my faith that real? I need the stories of other believers to reaffirm my own faith. I need to recall the sureness of the times God touched me in some way to feel confident of His love and guidance. Before the disease I was usually optimistic and enthusiastic. Illness seemed almost to take that away from me. It is a spiritual and emotional struggle to regain and retain joy and enthusiasm. Were they

my special gifts? Now can I better understand people who do not have that particular gift, but have others? By nearly taking it away from me, is God teaching me to appreciate and understand more?

With my illness, the opportunities are more frequent and more urgent for both receiving and giving. Trust and closeness with my family and friends is a gift that comes from weathering a storm together. The only way my negatives can become positive is to accept where I am.

Sometimes I feel like I am on a treadmill—going back and forth, trying to stay on my feet, but going nowhere— an endurance contest.

Then I remember where I am supposed to go. Not somewhere else. Right here! I only have to be here, helping my family and friends know they are loved and important. I am not alone unless I choose solitude and despair. Even in illness, I have someone I can touch, or some niche where I can give love, perhaps to someone no one else can reach.

June 1985

I thought I was all through with resentment and self-pity. I have lived with my disease for so long and people said I have such a good attitude. But I get tired of the problems, tired of myself, tired of repeated infections and tired of blood clots, tired of bowel obstructions and emergency runs to the hospital. I am tired of canes and IVs and medications and little daily aches and big debilitating pains.

Yet I realize that what I do with my body and my time is not up to my doctors. I control some things about my life. It is up to me to find helpful things each day.

The mountain-top experiences do not seem as frequent as the walks through the valley. I need those mountain tops for my vision and my hope, but I guess it is in the valleys that I meet the obstacles that strengthen me.

Birth and death, health and illness, valleys and mountains—all have lessons, beauties and dangers. I don't want to be pitied, nor forgotten, nor condemned, nor excused. I still have some things to learn and something to give. My need is greater now for the loving care of family and the care of God. But so is my opportunity greater.

❧

I can choose closeness, helpfulness, knowledge and gratitude. What good things can I find?

Bill's loving arms around me.

My dog's devotion and wagging tail.

Holding my grandchildren and noticing their soft skin, bright eyes and newly opening minds.

Walking, feeling the wind, looking at the sky, inhaling deep breaths.

Reading a good book, either something inspiring or something to escape.

Listening to the classical music I like best.

Working in my garden and harvesting enough to give some away.

Talking with my children, in person or on the phone.

How many good things can I pile up in one day?

❧

August 1985

I wonder, does God ever appear or speak to us in our modern world—does He guide us as He did the people in Biblical times? Or are we too busy or too sophisticated to think He does? I think I feel His guidance lots of times:

> *Not by giving in and giving up . . . but by inquiring and looking up.*
>
> *Not by building walls . . . but by building bridges.*
>
> *Not by shutting out relationships and friends to 'go it alone' . . . but by enriching my relationships and enlarging my community of helpers.*
>
> *Not by hiding myself from others . . . but by using all the resources I can muster, both internal and external.*
>
> *Not with bitterness . . . but with hope.*
>
> *Not by seeing cancer as a disaster . . . but as a challenge.*

Hospice

Birth and death, our coming and going from this world, are special times. Both should be full of warmth, love, happiness and reverence. Hospice is a program that provides both patient and family with what they most need as death is near. The goals are *comfort* when there is no cure; *control* of pain, *care* for both patient and family, and *help* for the bereaved family. Hospice provides special help ranging from assistance with care, household and children, to fun times with a special friend. Just the presence of a caring person to hold a hand may be a high priority. The program's purpose is to help provide patient and family with as much time as possible free from pain and worry so that their limited time can be spent with those they love. Hospice requires a community of caring people to cooperate, plan and secure this special care. Medical help, skilled help and volunteer help are all necessary components.

When the hospice concept was first publicized, many doubts were expressed that such a program was needed in Waseca County. Our county nurses were already caring for patients far beyond what was happening in many areas. However, joining the Minnesota Hospice organization in my dual capacity as social worker and as a cancer patient, I attended all the hospice conferences that were held in our area. To build up educational resources and education about hospice, we invited many people to attend our yearly professional education conferences. From 1982 to 1985, an average attendance of 200 people were stimulated by speakers who covered the subjects: Changing Concepts in Cancer Care, Interacting with the Patient in Pain, Finding Peace in Troubled Times, and Is Survival Always the Goal.

Another important fact to share was that cancer patients did not have to experience the pain that most of us feared. A Minnesota American Cancer Society committee developed a series of six programs: *Cancer and the Elderly.*[12] Two of the most innovative portions dealt with Pain Control and Comfort and Care. I presented this slide series at in-service programs in most of the hospitals and nursing homes in southern Minnesota. It is now available in video format from the American Cancer Society division in each state.

The Director of Nursing at Waseca Memorial Hospital conducted a "needs assessment" to survey families of all patients who died in our county over a three-year period. From the Professional Education committee, I delegated three nurses to develop a training program for volunteers. It was easy to gather enthusiasm and cooperation from our vigorous Make Today Count group. But soon the whole community became involved—hospital staff, nurses and doctors, ministers, funeral directors and social workers. The Waseca Hospice officially began in 1984 and continues to be strong.

Death: A Difficult Topic to Discuss

Our family went along doing the necessary things like eating meals together, but I did not really know how they felt about my cancer. Just sitting side by side did not provide osmosis for feelings to be transmitted. After reading in Elizabeth Kubler-Ross's books about the five stages of adjustment to loss and death, I asked Bill what he thought. When he said he did not want to talk about that, I was devastated and angry. It had taken a lot of courage for me to ask the question. Only after thinking and praying about it did I realize we were not emotionally at the same place regarding my cancer. With all the procedures I had experienced, my acceptance was at a different place than his. Bill needed more time.

A teacher in Chaska, Minnesota, asked me to speak about death to her health education class and requested I bring a family member along. To prepare for this, I wrote down several questions and asked our children and Bill to discuss them with me. We sat around the kitchen table, Paul and his wife Lynn, Dan and his wife Sara, and Patti. I told them I had questions that were important to me, and I wanted to know how they felt. It was still too difficult for Bill to talk openly about his feelings and he did not join us. Our youngest son Bob and I planned to talk on the drive back to his college the next day. This discussion with our children was tremendously important and their answers were not always what I expected.

Here are the questions I asked:

1. What did you feel when you were first told I had cancer? Were you angry, scared, stunned, unbelieving, what?

2. What did you do with that feeling? What is the first thing you did?

3. How do you feel now?

4. Is it hard or easy for you to talk about my illness?

5. Would you like me to talk less about it, or more? Do you want to hear about each medical consultation? I need to tell someone; should it be you?

6. Would you like more information about the nature of my illness?

7. Do you believe or think my disease is still active, cured, controlled, terminal?

8. As a result of experiences with my illness, are you more or less comfortable with death?

9. Did the realization that I might die occur to you?

10. Do you feel there has been anything positive that has come from living with me and my illness? What negative or difficult feelings have come to you while living with this illness in the family?

11. What activities would you like to do before death occurs?

12. Does it matter to you where death occurs—at home, nursing home, or hospital?

13. Who are the people to be notified in case of death?

14. What are your preferences about "life support" systems?

15. What are your preferences about body donations?

16. What are your preferences about funeral arrangements, songs to be sung, pallbearers, etc.?

I was hoping my body might have some scientific value, but no way did any of them want to donate my body to science. Eyes OK, but not the rest of me. When I asked whether I should talk more or less about my illness, Sara began to cry. With alarm, I asked if this was too difficult for her, since her mother died of cancer just a few years ago.

"That's not it," said Sara. "I'm crying because I wish we had talked with my mother like this. I am the oldest child and there were so many things I wished I knew when I had to help my Dad take care of my younger brother and sisters."

During the question "Did the realization that I might die occur to you?" Paul said,

"Yes, your dying was a thought that occurred to me, but Mom, you always taught us that life is a gift and when you're given a gift it's not polite to ask for more."

The next day, Bill decided to drive with us as I drove Bob back to college. He got caught up in the conversation, too. The day after he commented, "That was really a good talk we had yesterday."

It took all my courage to initiate that conversation about what cancer meant in our lives, but afterwards I was so glad I had done so. I told my Make Today Count friends about it and gave them my list of questions. Mabel, a very forthright and assertive person, wanted the same sort of discussion for her family of seven children. She asked if I would come to her house some evening when she could get the family all together. It wasn't until I was on the way to her house that I began to get cold feet and wondered what I was getting into.

Sixteen family members sat around the room while I asked the questions. A daughter-in-law spoke up saying, "I married your son because I love him and I love you, too. I felt left out when all of your children were called in at the time of your diagnosis, but the rest of us were not. I'm so glad, Mother, that you invited all of us to come tonight." There were many such moments of warmth and understanding before the evening was over.

Later, when Mabel was in the hospital as death neared, she said to me,

"I want to be sure you are there for my funeral. It will be my final party! Will you promise to come?"

"Of course I will."

She continued, "I feel very comfortable now about the readiness of all my family except my nine-year-old grandson. He doesn't say much."

Just at that moment, the grandson came in the door, carrying a fishing rod, with a small fish still dangling from it.

"I want to share my fish with you, Grandma. I wanted you to see it before we cook it. I'll bring some back in just a little while."

As he left the room, a smile spread across Mabel's face. She said, "Now I know he's OK too."

Untimely talk of retirement arrangements

My decreasing health gave extra urgency and importance to considerations Bill and I were giving to retirement. The words of one of the conference speakers provided guidance for the decision we were to make in the near future. Chaplain Howard Bell said, "In the last part of life, put yourself in a nurturing environment."

"Someday," said Bill in casual conversation with our realtor neighbor, "we may want a buyer for our house." We had observed the retirement arrangements of our parents, and we both felt that in our elder years (not now, of course), we would move to a retirement community where our health care and comfort were planned and secure. But we had just completed ten years of hard work finishing and landscaping our home, so now we were ready to relax and enjoy it without major projects to consume time, energy and money.

When Bill came home and told me, "We are show-ing the house tomorrow. We have a buyer who wants the house in three months for a family wedding," he was totally unprepared for my response. Instead of being his usually compliant wife, I stamped my feet, pounded the table and cried. I felt my nest was being whisked out from under me and my temper flared.

Visitors from Mexico

Show the house? Minor detail that we had some very special guests with us, a family of six from Valle De Bravo, Mexico. Our church had given continuous support to a literacy program founded by a missionary from our church. It was important for newer, younger members of the congregation to become acquainted with the project, so we invited Pepe and Aurea Vera-Cruz (who were carrying on this work) and their four Spanish-speaking boys to come to Waseca for three weeks. I was enjoying the visit immensely, but I was stretched to the limit struggling to speak Spanish and arranging meals and transportation.

What fun we had as I chauffeured them around town to visit the schools, hospital, senior center, churches and, perhaps most impressive to them, our county jail. As county attorney, Bill arranged for them to eat a meal in jail, for it was in the jail that they held a number of their classes in reading and arithmetic. Their tutoring enabled many released prisoners to earn a living in-stead of begging and stealing. They were accustomed to concrete tables set upon a dirt floor where they taught inmates enough reading and math to find work.

A good Minnesota snowstorm came on the first Saturday of their visit, a beautiful one, covering the trees and the ground with a soft blanket. On Sunday after church, we were deluged by friends bringing boots, jackets, stocking caps, sleds and tricycles. The older boys, Pepito, 16, Ricardo, 13, and Fredrico, 11, knew instinctively how to make snowballs and what to do with them. Not so, little 4-year-old Jaime, who objected vigorously to the cumbersome mittens we put on his hands.

It was in the midst of this busy time that Bill announced the realtor wanted to show the house. I wanted to make no such major change in our life and refused to discuss it until after our guests had gone. The last morning, after friends took them to the airport at 5 a.m., I took Nicky, my big German shepherd, for a long walk. We hiked across the golf course and into the woods. There I sat on a log and meditated. I prayed and I listened for God's will to be made known. How long would I live with my cancer? How much care would I need in the future? Was this the time to give up the house? Were any of the retirement communities where I wanted to be? How long were the waiting lists? What should we do? Where was that "nurturing environment" the chaplain said we should seek?

An hour or two passed as I talked to myself, to my dog and to my God. I left the woods and headed for home. Bill was standing on the deck. He called out to me "What have you decided?"

Sometime ago Bill and I discussed where we would want to live when the time came that one of us was alone. We agreed it would be Covenant Manor, a retirement community in Minneapolis. But now? So soon? I certainly did not want to move. We would probably have to live somewhere else temporarily, rent a house in town. No way! Unless, somehow, we could move directly from home to retirement, I did not want to sell.

I made a phone call to one of the retirement places we had considered.

"Yes, we can get you in. You've thought long enough; come up and we'll sign the papers," said an abrasive pushy voice of the saleswoman. Whoa, not so fast! I was already feeling pushed; don't shove me!

Then I called Covenant Manor and was greeted by a considerate voice that said,

"This has come up faster than you expected. It is a big decision. We will need to call you back, but we will do everything we can to help you make a decision that is right for you."

Here we found our "nurturing environment." Compassion, friendship, totally independent living now, with total care available when needed. On July 1, 1985, we moved from our lovely home in Waseca to an equally lovely retirement home in the Minneapolis suburb called Golden Valley.

Traveling in retirement

Part of our retirement plan included some traveling. Camping had been our family's vacation style. The out of doors called us more than the shows and artifices of man-made entertainment. Since a tent no longer supplied our needs for creature comforts, we had a "fifth-wheel" travel trailer built to our specifications: a taller ceiling and longer bed for 6'4" Bill, lots of storage for our hobbies, and a "slide out" living room for extra space. After selling our house, we moved our furniture to Minneapolis, but we lived in the trailer from July to November while Bill completed his work at the law office. We parked the trailer 13 miles from Waseca on the shores of Lake Sakatah, next to the motel owned by Patti and Greg, who had moved back to Minnesota from California. Once a week I drove to Minneapolis to unpack a box or two in our apartment and have lunch at Covenant Manor.

With the first snowfall, we hitched the trailer to our truck and drove to Cloud Nine Ranch in Southern Missouri. We belonged to a family campground near West Plains; we could safely leave the trailer there over the winter months. Over the next seven years, we traveled to Florida to visit our son Bob, who worked at Disney

World; to Tucson, Arizona, to visit my brother; and to the New England states. We traveled up the coast to Nova Scotia and took a ferry to Prince Edward Isle in the fall when the bright red of the maple trees was punctuated by dark green evergreen spires.

From Texas to Canada we explored at a leisurely pace. I carried a letter from my doctor, which gave recommendations for emergency treatment. Most trips required some medical care serious enough to need a doctor's help. We carried a CB in the truck to call for help. When we camped in a new area, as on previous trips, the first thing we did was to find the hospital emergency entrance. Then we made a "dry run" so we wouldn't get confused if we had to go there in the middle of the night.

I always checked in with my doctor before leaving. Before one trip she looked me over and said "You're leaving, but not on a trip. You're going to the hospital." I was put into isolation with viral meningitis. After leaving the hospital, headaches persisted for a long time. I walked in the woods at the campground, wondering if my head would ever feel OK again.

Before another trip, I checked with the doctor about a small irritating rash on my back. Shingles! Not unusual for lymphoma patients, and it was caught early. We left on our trip armed with medication, pain killers and tegaderm bandages.

While we were on another camping trip, we needed medical advice for a high fever and lethargy. Bill called on our CB radio to reach the camp's emergency medical technicians. They recommended an immediate trip to the hospital, either by helicopter or by car. Bill drove me to the hospital where the doctor diagnosed pneumonia and prescribed antibiotics. We learned to take all of this in stride. Travel was far more fun than staying home waiting to be better, when we knew this was as "better" as I'd get. I was learning to live!

One day the American Cancer Society called me to refer another patient who wanted to travel and wondered what precautions to take. I shared my check list.

❧ My Checklist for Travel ❧

1. First, check with the doctor about where I'm going and how I'm doing.
2. Ask the doctor for a letter to any medical personnel I may need to see en route.
3. Ask the doctor for advice or names of approved clinics in the area to which I'll be traveling.
4. Ask for prescriptions sufficient to cover expected needs.
5. Ask the pharmacist to fill my prescriptions with sufficient quantity to cover the trip and a week extra. Ask about phoning for additional medications if necessary.
6. Wear an identification or "medic-alert" bracelet.
7. Carry a list of medications and a brief medical history.
8. Carry information about medical and hospital insurance.
9. Plan itinerary before leaving home. Make reservations in advance. Give a copy to family members.
10. Have a plan for keeping in touch with family members, and do so regularly. We use our telephone answering machine.
11. Locate the hospital emergency entrance at every overnight stop.
12. Ask what CB channel is monitored by camp staff where we are staying. Make a test call.
13. Continue with prayer and daily devotions while traveling.
14. Spend more time enjoying than worrying.

Use your mind to help your body.

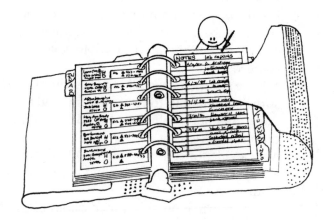

Knowledge is power.
Knowledge dilutes fear.

8

Using Mind/Body Connections

When I first felt I was getting lost in the cracks of medical care, I began to keep a journal. Many different doctors treated me in hospital emergency rooms, so I bought a little blue book in which I recorded what was done when and where. I wrote questions as they occurred to me. I took my journal with me into the doctor's office. This prompted me and gave me courage to ask questions. I wrote the doctor's answers and repeated them back before I left to ensure that we understood each other accurately.

Cancer was not just a minor illness that would go away by itself. I was treading on unstable ground with BIG pitfalls. Did I know what was important and what was not?

The only way to be secure in this threatening territory was to trust my doctors and give them all the information they needed. Skilled as they were, medical people had no psychic powers to know all my doubts and experiences. I had to make my needs known. I needed to listen carefully and follow through accurately on doctor's evaluations and directions. Sometimes I wrote lists, or graphs, or charts. On numerous occasions my doctor and I reviewed my notes together and came to conclusions aided by my documentation.

Memories, especially painful ones, tended to flatten out with time. My journal helped me remember clearly. I appreciated both my own strengths and the strengths of those who helped me. With a serious illness there are many moments of deep thought—spiritual—grateful—resentful. These thoughts, too, went into my journal. It was not quite like a diary, for I recorded both facts and feelings. When I looked back, I was often surprised at the clarity of a problem and the problem's solution. I could see where I had been and rejoice at my progress. Journaling also provided opportunity for contemplation when I looked ahead to determine goals. Its many-faceted purposes included documenting information so I would not forget—and releasing frustrations so I *could* forget!

When I was very sick, I did not feel like writing, but I found another journaling technique that was equally effective. I had a small book of sayings, some inspirational, some funny, some practical. Reading these short passages took little effort. I found myself either agreeing or disagreeing with what was printed. Then I'd put an exclamation mark or a question mark in the margin. Or I'd wrote "Hurray, that is right,"—"No, it's not that way,"—"I need to learn," or whatever was appropriate.

My journal was organized like this—

1. On the inside cover of the record book I wrote all phone numbers important to my health: doctor, hospital, pharmacy, cancer society, health insurance, social security number, telephone credit number, and family phone numbers. I also scotch taped an air ambulance brochure, in case I should have to fly home.

2. On the first page I wrote my diagnosis, dates of CT scans, X-rays, lab tests, date and place of hospitalizations, surgeries, implants and emergency room visits.

3. I listed all medications, strength and frequency—also all medications taken as needed (PRN)—both prescription and across the counter drugs and why I took them.

4. For easy reference, I recorded lab reports and doctor appointments at the top right hand page throughout the journal.

5. I dated each journal entry where I recorded feelings and questions. In the margin I put a "?" beside those I wanted to ask the doctor, leaving space to write the answer in a different colored ink.

6. I kept the book in a handy place. I took it to the doctor's office and carried it while traveling.

I did not write every day, but I wrote frequently, especially during times of discouragement or encouragement. I had no idea when I started this journey that the way would be so long and winding, with hills and valleys, twists and turns. Journaling helped me find my way. I carried on imaginary conversations with myself or with those I loved, whether with me or not. I wrote in public or in private, for five minutes or for an hour, in bed or while traveling. Studies have been done that indicate journaling actually promotes healing. This uncomplicated act is as individual as a fingerprint, as revealing as a microscope, and as poignant as a tear. I was fascinated to learn that something so simple promotes wellness!

A puzzling syndrome

The puzzling and painful syndrome that began four years ago continued to occur frequently with twinges of discomfort, building up to spasms of intense pain. I felt pain and pressure like childbirth labor, only there was no baby. After five or six hours, I heaved up stomach contents, then intestinal contents. My insides churned, forcefully ejecting large amounts of acidic, smelly fluid with small chunks of formed feces. I felt like I was somersaulting off a cliff just before I lost consciousness and collapsed into a convulsive seizure, and quit breathing. Fortunately, Bill was trained in CPR; he shook me, called my name and forced his breath into my mouth. I awoke exhausted.

"Small bowel obstructions," said my doctor. "Your small intestine is locked down. Radiation made it rigid and inflexible. Gas, food, liquid gets trapped in the folds of the small intestine. It is serious, can be life-threatening from a build up of toxins. Get into a hospital emergency room when it happens," he said.

We made many a harried and difficult run to the nearest hospital emergency room just before or just following these episodes. I was admitted to the hospital on the average of once a week for drugs administered by injection, rehydration by IV, and sometimes a nasal gastric tube.

Imagery

How could I handle these episodes of pain so intense that I vomited my insides out and lost consciousness? Doctors said surgery would make it worse. The damage was done and was irreparable. In my desperate efforts to survive, I stumbled into Imagery, although I did not know at the time that it had a name. Without the benefit of medical guidance, I began to practice self-hypnosis and imagery. I did not realize how effective it was until I heard a doctor in the emergency room of a hospital in St. Petersburg, Florida, ask my husband if I was taking something to make me sleepy. I heard the question but could not allow anything to penetrate my semi-hypnotic state. All my effort was required to maintain a controlled state of relaxation to dull the pain.

This process was given credibility and a name when I heard Dr. Karen Olness speak at a conference about her studies in behavioral research to help children control pain. With practice in biofeedback, imagery and self-hypnosis, children learned to monitor and control their pain perceptions. I was very excited and stimulated to hear that what I had been doing was medically possible, permissible *and* beneficial.

Researchers were also reporting that the use of TENS stimulated endorphin production. My past experience of using a TENS unit for pain probably helped my body learn how to increase its own pain killers.

I had a lot of practice between the years of 1978 and 1987. Rather than tensing and fighting the spasms, I tried to relax and let the pain wash over and beyond me. The most relaxing place I could think of was the weightlessness of my body under water. As a certified scuba diver, I mentally placed myself under water, breathing easily and slowly through my regulator, my body floating freely with the rhythm of underwater currents in an area of serene beauty. Sights, sounds, smells and every sense were brought into play in using imagery.

Late one night in 1987, I woke up and stretched to relieve a kink in my side. I went to the bathroom and crawled back into bed before I realized that pronounced pain came with each breath I took. I wondered if a new blood clot in my leg could have broken loose and traveled. I breathed a prayer, "Help me relax and go back to sleep, dear God, or wake my husband if I need care." Bill woke up!

The next four hours included phone calls to the doctor, a quick trip to the hospital, X-rays, EKG, lung scan and blood tests. I was suffering from a pulmonary embolism, with more than one clot caught in my lungs.

Statistically one-third of pulmonary embolisms cause death. In about 70 percent of that one-third, death occurs within the first hour, usually because a clot interferes with blood flow between the heart and lungs. Had I not been in the intensive care unit (ICU), connected to what I called the "power tower" that monitored my body systems, the crisis would not have been discovered and averted in time to save my life. When I heard a warning alarm sound, I glanced at the monitor that showed my heart was pulsing at 39 beats per minute. The next sensation was like sinking into a bubbling dark pool, and I lost consciousness. My next awareness was that a flurry of people were in the room and something hit my chest, hard. When Bill came to see me, he told me I'd had a cardiac arrest.

Here is Bill's story of that event:

Marvyl has told you she had had countless bowel blockages. We were in an emergency room of some hospital on an almost a once-a-week frequency for more than a two-year period. The blockages came on with slowly-advancing pain and disability. More times than I want to recall, they resulted in vomiting and unconsciousness, often with the result that Marvyl would cease breathing. Sometimes her fingernails and her lips began to turn blue. Six or eight times I resorted to mouth-to-mouth resuscitation—something we had both learned so Marvyl could help me when I "—had my heart attack—" and other times I shook her or slapped her to get her breathing again.

When Marvyl awoke complaining of a sharp pain in her back at the base of her lungs, we both realized from prior experience that this possibly could be a pulmonary embolism. We raced to the hospital emergency room where the emergency doctor was sufficiently concerned to call in a specialist even in those wee hours of the morning. The specialist ordered Marvyl to the cardiac floor. I heard him tell the nurses to get her into "a monitored bed." I knew what that meant from prior experience. They put on the electrodes, and by a radio device sent the bodily system information to a central monitoring station, sometimes a long way down the hall. The doctor left. Time was consumed. There was no monitored bed available. The nurses conferred. I think they were concerned about calling the doctor with the news at that early hour. They made the decision themselves. They told me they were having her placed in an intensive care unit (ICU) until a monitored bed opened up. I would have been extremely worried (I do a lot of that about her) if she first had been ordered into ICU.

In ICU only close relatives could visit and then only for 10 minutes during each two hours. I have been in so many hospitals with Marvyl that I guess I naturally bend the rules. I was trying to sneak in 30 minutes early when one of the ICU nurses stopped me. "We are working with your wife. You must wait."

So, OK, I figured they were changing her gown or the bed linen or something like that.

I came back to get my 10-minute visit, this time per the rules. The nurse again stopped me. "Mr. Patton, I have something to show you." With that she pulled about five feet of an EKG strip out of Marvyl's chart. At the beginning were a few small "blips," each successive one getting smaller and then dear Lord!—just a flat line.

"Your wife has suffered a complete cardiac arrest. We had to resuscitate her. You may see her for just a moment. She is under sedation now."

Until you go through it yourself, I do not think you can understand the shock of that display and those words. She had many close calls, but—

About two hours later, I was in the waiting room. Dr. Bowers interrupted what had been almost constant prayer. This empathetic and compassionate lady who had done so much for Marvyl was grinning—no other word for it—she was GRINNING. How inappropriate! Here my wife had been clinically dead and her doctor looked like she was celebrating!

"Bill, we know why she does it! We know why she does it!" I distinctly remember she said it twice. "We know why Marvyl stops breathing when she is under acute pain, and we know how to stop it! This time it happened when she was monitored and the tape tells us!" Doctor Bowers explained that under acute pain her vagus nerve just retreats and no longer stimulates the node or nodes that cause the heart to beat. A pacemaker would assure it would not happen again.

If I had not been there every time to shake or slap or give mouth-to-mouth, Marvyl would just have slipped away from me. If there had been a monitored bed available, it would have been touch and go whether resuscitation could have been made in time. If— If— Thank you so much, Lord God!

❦

After consultation with a cardiologist, Dr. Bowers recommended a pacemaker implant to stimulate my heart when it slowed and thus prevent another arrest. When she told me, I resisted the idea. Cancer was enough. I did not want to have heart problems, too! She explained that the heart muscle itself was not diseased. It was just the signal to beat that was weak under trauma. Later that day a nurse from the heart unit came to explain the pacemakers. The kind recommended for me would permit my nerves and heart to function normally. Only if the beat slowed down would the pacemaker "kick in." It was a preventative measure, needed only intermittently. With some reluctance I agreed to the time set for surgery.

The cardiologist came into the surgical suite whistling the "Toreador Song" from Carmen. That delighted me. I was prepped, swabbed, draped and injected with pain killers for the implant of the pacemaker. I asked that the monitor be moved into position where I could watch. I saw the lead inserted into my vein, steered to my heart, retracted a bit and repositioned in just the right place in the ventricle of my beating heart. Amazing!

Back in my room I was instructed to lie immobilized on my back for 36 hours. As the medication wore off, the combined pain of the embolism and the surgical implant increased. I expected some discomfort—say about "two to three" on a scale of "one to ten." But my pain increased to a "seven." Could I transfer my knowledge of handling abdominal pain to controlling chest pain?

I tried to place myself in a weightless condition under water, but the pain stayed intense. I mentally put on a wet suit jacket that was too tight, constricting my shoulder and chest, as I imaged myself under water. No good.....it hurt!

I concentrated on increasing the endorphins to diminish the pain. No luck.

I wrapped myself, figuratively, in cotton batting, suspending myself inside its comforting softness. It was better momentarily, but I could not hold the image long enough.

I did the usual exercises of progressive relaxation. I concentrated on the rhythm of breathing.

I imagined myself on a beach, lying on the sand in the sun. Over the area of pain, I pretended I was sun burned. Not much good. So I imagined I plunged into the water, felt the coolness on my chest, rolled over on my back and took some strenuous back strokes, stretching and reaching, feeling the pull on my chest and shoulders and then relaxing and floating awhile. That helped, but I could not hold that image very long either. I wanted more relief.

As I looked in the mirror opposite my bed, I felt like I was seeing a helpless gray insect strapped down by ten tubes holding me in place. I had a urinary catheter; an IV in each arm; an oxygen tube in my nose; a heat pump attached to a wet pad on my arm, where an IV infiltrated; and a heart monitor hanging heavy on my chest with four electrodes attached. I was immobilized except for my antennae—the antennae on the little gray bug, which it seemed was me, were moving and probing ceaselessly, testing each cranny of memory, each nook of past experience, each potential crack of hope, trying to find somewhere I could be comfortable—some little niche or piece of experience to help with my discomfort and pain.

What could I draw on from past experience to help me with the present pain? Had I ever experienced similar pain that I'd managed successfully? I traveled backwards through my life and recalled nursing my children—the discomfort of breast engorgement—a delicious feeling of purposefulness with the "let down" reflex, the pulling and tightening and tingling as that tiny mouth suckled, the easing of fullness and discomfort as the baby withdrew milk from my breast. What a miracle! What a wonder was that little body, so recently a part of me ......That was it!

I could relive and sustain those memories. I re-imaged every little detail: awaking to discomfort, hearing the small baby sounds turn to crying, picking up the tiny, warm body and carrying him to the changing table. I recalled the sweet smell of new-born baby wet warmth, the yellow color and spicy smell of breast milk stool. I felt tiny fingers curl around mine. I felt his soft skin.

I went on and on, imaging myself back in that time, prolonging the image, enriching it with more details, sustaining it and finding ease from my present pain. Not total absence of pain, of course! I knew I was 64 years old and in a hospital for pulmonary embolism and pacemaker implant, but I could control the images in my mind, fill it with the lesser pain and pleasure of a time gone by. I unlocked a memory, drew it out, stretched it, and used it to comfort my hurting body!

My hospital roommate listened as I told her about my experience. In her present state of fear and pain she wished she could talk with her mother, hear her words of comfort, but her mother had died several years ago. I encouraged her to let her mind take her back to her mother, remember her in every detail, create an image and a conversation with her. She tried it and found it a tremendous help. She was surprised how much her pain and fear were minimized by recalling past conversations with her mother and feeling the comfort of her presence.

One of my nurses suggested that I document my experiences for others who wanted to learn about imagery. My training in medical social work gave me opportunities to work with patients and with health professionals, both individually and as a speaker at conferences. From notes recorded in my journal and an extensive perusal of professional literature on the topic, I wrote the following program.

❧❦❧

USING IMAGERY FOR PAIN CONTROL

Reviving Knowledge from the Past

Before science discovered the "wonder drugs," the "hypos" and the anesthetics to relieve pain, primitive man used the tools of imagery and self-hypnosis. Until recently they were belittled or forgotten. Now medical science is taking another look and discovering that we do have unused powers within our own minds to help our bodies.

These tools no longer come to us automatically because we haven't used them. Just as it is possible to strengthen a muscle with exercise or to stimulate a salivary gland by thinking about it, it is possible to acquire skill in manufacturing and releasing necessary body chemicals.

Important Precepts

There are several precepts I feel are very important in understanding the use of imagery:

1. The image works best when it is something within the patient's experience. Fantasizing an image (such as inhaling tiny polar bears or pac men to gobble up cancer cells) is effective for some, but my personal experience is that reality is more powerful. Diving under the water certainly wouldn't calm everyone, as

it does me. Perhaps some would prefer walking on a beautiful golf course or racing on roller blades.

2. All senses should be drawn into the imagery to make it most effective: smelling, tasting, hearing, seeing, touching and emotional feeling.

3. All images do not have to be pleasant ones. Draw on the experience of successfully living through a previous painful experience.

4. Others may help patients use imagery techniques, whether or not the patient is aware of how the process works.

Just as the physical therapist uses exercises to help in gaining muscle strength, similar exercises will help with learning to manage pain. It is important to use any exercise program for a period of time before results can be felt. Too often patients rely wholly on their expectations of what the doctor or therapist will do for them, without realizing the importance of what they can do for themselves.

Structured Exercises Using Imagery to Control Pain

Health professionals or family members may direct the patient or, better yet, patients themselves may take responsibility for doing these exercises.

1. Squeeze your salivary glands to make more "juice." You can do it without knowing exactly how those glands work. Practice doing it. Now think of other glands in your body. Some of them produce endorphins to help control pain. Think about them several times a day and see if your mind can stimulate them just as it did the salivary glands.

2. Pinch the fleshy part of your thumb with your fingernail until you feel pain. When it is hurting a bit, say over and over again, "Relax, Relax, Relax." As you

think about relaxing, the pressure is automatically lessened and the pain diminishes.

3. Bite your tongue or your cheek. This requires some tension and pressure from the jaw muscles. Pain is often more intense due to tension or pressure. Now say to yourself "Let go, let go, let go." When you are experiencing pain in your body, say over and over again "relax" or "let go." Say it out loud, or at least whisper it to yourself. Feel the pain subside as the tension is released.

4. Choose a certain time of day to concentrate on thinking good health. For example, every time you go outdoors take three deep lung filling breaths and think of inhaling health. Or when you gulp that first swallow of juice in the morning. One woman takes a spoonful of peanut butter once each day and while its in her mouth she thinks "make more white cells."

5. Experiment with ways of breathing. Make the abdomen rise with deep abdominal breathing. Do it at least five times. Make the chest rise with intercostal breathing—five times. Pant with each exhalation—five times. Open the mouth with each intake—five times. Blow out with each exhalation—five times. Determine which makes the pain less. Concentrate on the rhythm of this usually automatic process.

6. Practice isometric exercises to locate muscle systems and learn to identify a tense or a relaxed state. Practice progressive relaxation, with or without music or audio tapes.

7. Massage your face, forehead, cheeks and chin, going over the bony prominences several times. Have someone massage your feet, hands or back. Use a little lotion and take plenty of time.

8. Stretch the large muscles of arms and legs like a cat would, or have help from someone doing "range of motion" exercises. Do a pelvic rock in whatever posi-

tion is best for you: lying in bed, kneeling, sitting or standing.

9. Deliberately look for and find a situation, or a joke, or a videotape that causes you to laugh, deep tummy-jiggling laughter. Friends can help a lot here by bringing you stories or jokes. Some people fear it is inappropriate to laugh while stricken with a serious illness. Instead, it is one of the best things you can do for both mind and body. Develop occasions for hearty laughter.

10. Think about whatever is a favorite activity or place. Recall as much as possible about how it looks, feels, smells, sounds. Keep adding to it with more details. Find a place where you are engrossed in what you are doing and enjoying. Stay there as long as possible.

My experience with acute pain required a conscious search. I examined and discarded many images before I found one that was helpful. It required real effort and concentration.

Structured Conversation: Caretakers

Recalling favorite activities is particularly useful for elderly people. Encourage remembering old times. Relive those memories. We all know we can sometimes forget our pain when engrossed in something we enjoy.

It is very important to acknowledge, and not belittle, the patient's pain. It is a personal feeling, which becomes more intense if others refuse to acknowledge it and its importance. Whatever the cause, pain is real for the person experiencing it.

Talk with the patients and ask whether they are more comfortable with window drapes and doors open or closed. Some want to withdraw and be away from the world. Others find that dark and quiet create a sense of isolation, loneliness or fear of being forgotten.

Consider the kind of music the patient likes: classical, easy listening, country western, etc. Keep a radio within reach, tuned in to the right station, so the patient can find it when wakeful in the middle of the night or anytime he is feeling pain.

Consider whether the patient wants to hear the noises of children playing, household activity, people coming and going in the hospital or nursing home. Some do not want to be shut out and isolated. Others want to be left alone. Incorrectly assuming the patient's preference leaves him feeling out of control and may contribute to intensifying both fear and pain.

Consider whether touching is part of the patient's emotional milieu. Hand holding, patting, rubbing, hugging can be either reassuring or aggravating. If pain is intense, I like my hand quietly held, but do not want the jarring effect of rubbing or patting.

Verbal Encouragement: Patients

Explore possibilities. It is possible to minimize pain by thoughts and activities. Unfamiliar terms like self-hypnosis, biofeedback and imagery do not mean a scary procedure where our control is taken away. Rather, we enhance our ability to take control. A hurting body needs both medical skills and self skills to function most effectively.

Practice these self skills. Like the training of a fine musician or an Olympic athlete, consistent practice can accomplish seemingly impossible feats. Even relaxation can be developed to Olympic proportions! Modifications are possible for any of the above exercises to accommodate the ambulatory and the bedridden.

Some patients have neither the physical nor the psychological capacity to actively "work" on pain control. However, some of the techniques described may be used even without a patient's awareness, with a degree of success still achieved. Ideally both patient and caregiver are aware of the goal of lessening pain, will discuss the methods used, and will gain confidence with success.

Accept individual differences

It is tremendously important to avoid instilling a feeling of guilt or failure if the patient's work is unproductive. Sometimes the disease process is too great to be overcome. Even then, it is important to muster all forces and use them as advantageously as possible. It is common knowledge that medical skills, nursing interventions and medications are more effective with a cooperative patient.

Trying a new procedure only once or twice may not work. The organs and cells of the body work in a slow and rhythmic fashion. Repeated practice is necessary and new problems require new skills. Healthy cells are more amazing than science fiction in their intricacy and capacity. The traditional view of cancer as a foreign crab eating away and destroying organs and bones is an inaccurate illustration with negative connotations. A more accurate and less frightening description of cancer is that the body's own cells do not mature properly. Cancer cells are like teenagers who are delinquent, pushing and shoving their way before they have fully matured—not taking responsibility for the work they are supposed to do—running around where they don't belong—reproducing too freely—gobbling up all the food—and not obeying the rules. Rather than big bad germs, they are defective, immature cells.

Nearly everyone can learn and practice some new techniques to help when there is pain or disease.

Some things are so important they are worth whatever the cost in fatigue or pain

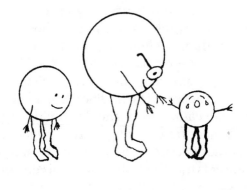

Allow memories of yesterday to help with today's pain.

9

Chances and Choices

It took a while for me to understand El Gallo's closing words in the musical play, *The Fantastiks*. "There must always be a wall."

It took a lifetime of growing to understand the spiritual "Please don't move that mountain."

It took a serious illness for me to understand that "Pain is inevitable, but misery is optional."

It took some deep thinking to realize there was more than poignancy in the anthem "Jesus Walked that Lonesome Valley."

It took surviving many trials and challenges to be convinced that "God's grace is sufficient in all circumstances."

These are widely divergent quotations from literature and song, but each is a facet of the same precious gem: *important lessons learned*.

The presence of a forbidding wall makes the treasures on the other side all the more desirable. It is our challenges that cause the need to struggle. It is the struggles that cause the need to grow, to seek, to learn. It is our difficulties that make us aware of our own weakness and our need to depend on God and others for help.

We are given the opportunity to choose, not always what happens to us in our lives, but which way we should go—around, over, under, through the obstacles. The old spiritual says, "Lord don't move that mountain. Lead me Lord around it." We, too, must walk that lonesome valley; nobody else can walk it for us.

Going around the mountain

Bill and I learned how to adjust to many crises, limiting our travel and activities in some directions, but leaving some options open.

One of the recurring troubles that continued to bother me was lack of control following a small bowel obstruction. For example, it was not unusual for a meal to trigger rapid emptying of the bowel without warning or any ability to control. This happened while shopping, while standing in conversation, and while dining at a beautiful restaurant. As quickly as possible, I would retreat to the privacy of a restroom stall, use many baby-wipes that I carry in my purse to sponge and mop to cleanliness, and put on a change of underwear, which I also carry for such emergencies. I always feel a bit shaky when I return and pretend nothing out of the ordinary has happened.

When I looked back on the sequence of events and their individual "horrors," major sickness seemed quite evident, but when I took one episode at a time, it seemed almost minor—inconvenient, but *not* impossible.

In my mother's generation, patients turned inward and became reclusive because there were no conveniences to help with embarrassing situations. They became smothered by the illness, secluded and excluded. No wonder cancer was feared as it cut off all the pleasant things of life. But that is not true today. Not for me! To be included, I put myself in the midst of people and absorbed joy and enthusiasm from them. I had two choices to make about my "embarrassing" accidents. I could either let them make me retire from society, feel tainted and inadequate, or I could use the pharmaceutical helps available, make adjustments and be with the people I enjoy. To be polite, I tried to cover up all that was not well and that I deemed unpleasant. Only with other patients could I share my feelings and be understood.

> *Concentration on the problem increases the discomfort, but denial makes pain even more potent. Acceptance of what is and conscious effort to find pleasure can minimize the pain.*

Both medical studies and patient stories espouse the value of acceptance and distraction in painful situations.

Our travels involved some risks and often medical intervention. But travel also provided fun and new experiences—*valuable* experiences—well worth the cost of whatever physical problems occurred. If, instead of worrying about what might happen, I concentrated on the pleasure of planning, doing and then remembering the fun times, they gave me pleasure enough to modify pain.

Choosing distractions

Everyone, even a person with chronic illness, has interests and hobbies that stimulate and give pleasure. If they don't, they should cultivate some. A patient friend said to me, "If I'd just get to feeling better, I would do those things again." Wrong. Wrong. Wrong. Turn the sentence around: "Do some of those things again and you will feel better."

All cancer patients won't have the same interests I have. Whatever once brought a light to *your* eye, a smile to *your* face, do it again. Modify the activity to accommodate your new physical status, but expose yourself to those joys. It sometimes seemed to me that doing that would be too much work or too impossible. I had to convince myself with a lot of self-talk, hope and trust that the effort would be worth it. I had one friend who would say, "Well, I'll never do that again. I ached all over the next day." So what! Didn't she enjoy the fact that she did it? Were some aches too high a price to pay for pleasure?

It is helpful to put yourself in the company of those who enjoy what you used to do, whether it is repairing old cars, playing football or competing in something you'll never do again.

Keep your consciousness at high level; be observant, store up memories, retell the stories, revel in the pictures, keep a log. Relive it. Enjoy it.

Relive it in your memories and take joy and comfort from the memory. Thinking about problems is only part of your life. You can also have many life-enhancing activities. They are part of you, too. You are not just cancer.

I cannot hike anymore. I don't get up early to go "birding," because I cannot stand or walk more than a few minutes. How could I still enjoy bird watching? To give you an example, I'll tell a story about one of my highlights—a Coming Out Party!

Every spring our friends, Walter and Dorothy Breckenridge, held a "coming out" party for the wood ducks that nest in their trees. The day after hatching, the downy little ducks tumbled out of the nest box and fell more than 15 feet to the ground. "Breck," a well-known wildlife artist and naturalist, invited us to view this rarely seen event at their home on a wooded stretch of the Mississippi River.

The alarm jangled to alert us to get there early. We drove a few miles before entering a driveway that penetrated deep into a woodland. We tried not to rustle and crackle anything underfoot, as we sneaked out of the car under mother duck's watchful eye. She was sitting, plump and patient, on top of the man-made wood duck house attached to a tree near the home.

Mother duck moved her head purposefully, surveying the ground beneath. "Perhaps she saw our reflections through the windows," said Breck. Pulling all the blinds and darkening the room added to the mystery and the expectancy. Some of us pulled the drapes apart only a little; others stretched their fingers in the slats of the venetian blinds.

After an hour passed, mother duck flew from the nest. "There!" said our host, "she now will fly into the nest box and coax the little ones out." Suddenly a neighbor child broke the spell, as he ran across the yard. Mother duck flew back to her perch on top of the nest box, ruffled her feathers and settled back to resume her patient watch. Again and again her head moved back and forth, back and forth, as she looked for any signs of danger beneath. We waited. Another hour passed.

"Look! She's off again...maybe this time—" She circled the area and quickly slipped through the hole in the nest box. "Now, she'll lead the little ones out," said Breck. We waited expectantly.

So quickly, so tiny we almost missed it, a little yellow brown ball of fluff tumbled out of the hole down to the ground. Immediately mother duck followed, sat beside her little one and called up to the others to follow.

The next little fellow poked his head out and teetered on the brink long enough for us to get a good look. He was so soft, fluffy and tiny that he looked like a toy you'd find in an Easter basket. Except, his dark little eye showed life and light. Whoops! There he went; a bit unsteady, he somersaulted as he went down.

Quickly, together, we all counted numbers as two - three - four tumbled out. Little five and six came to the doorway together. They seemed to float down, weighing next to nothing. In quick succession now they came. Each one had his own style of descent. Only one day old, they tumbled 15 feet down into a leafy green world, at the encouraging call of their mother and siblings. Little number eleven paused, looked around, and with a push of his tiny feet, he arched in the air with a graceful dive.

We were mesmerized by the drama we were watching. For only a couple of moments, the ducks were visible on the mowed lawn before they disappeared in the brushy steep slope going down to the river. A fleeting glimpse and they were gone.

Breck got a ladder to check the nest box to see about the twelfth egg. He said nothing, but came down and held out his hand and placed it in mine. The warmth of the twelfth egg he put in my hand was so silky smooth; it felt soft and wonderful. Instinctively, I put it next to my cheek.

"Peep, Peep," so strong and close to my ear it startled me. I moved it again. "Peep, Peep, Peep," came from within the egg. "Oh my, I'm about to become a mother duck," I cried. "What do I do?" I examined the egg; there was no crack yet. I passed it around. Eagerly and carefully, each hand, in turn, reached for a chance to hold it, to marvel at the tiny vulnerable life inside.

Mama and 11 ducklings had gone their way. There was no chance for "slowpoke" to find them and catch up. Sadly, but hopefully, we placed the living egg in a cloth-lined box to be carried to another nest, where we hoped he would be adopted.

Choosing to endure

As I hurried to a meeting at the American Cancer Society office in Minneapolis, the Executive, Harry Linduff passed by me in the hallway. He touched my shoulder and said "they" had just decided to send me to Washington, D. C. as Minnesota's representative at the 75-year celebration. "Sounds wonderful," I said casually, having no idea what was in store.

In March, 1988, Bill and I flew to the capital city to participate in three fabulous days of being treated like royalty——flowers, banquets, medals, accolades and TV interviews. Each year the American Cancer Society honors a dignitary (usually a movie star or well known personality) who has survived cancer and done notable public service. The president of the United States awards a Medal of Courage to that person. To mark the 75th year of progress in cancer control, the society decided to honor someone from each state to represent the five million cancer survivors. I was there to represent Min-

Kay Horsch and Marvyl Patton

nesota. There also were a few dignitaries "at large," making a total of 60 honorees. (Each year has shown a dramatic increase in the number of cancer survivors from 1.5 million when I was first diagnosed in 1973 to nearly 7 million in 1994.)

We arrived at the hotel and were greeted by the National Chairman of the Board, Kay Horsch, from Minneapolis. Around my neck she placed a red, white and blue ribbon with an Olympic-style medal bearing the insignia "Celebration of Life." She entertained the Midwest cancer survivors and families at a small coffee hour so we could get acquainted before going to an elegant banquet in the hotel dining room.

At the banquet, each guest of honor was pictured on two large screens for all to see. The video presentation was called "Faces of Courage" and a short vignette of each person's history was given. We were given our packets of information and schedules for the three-day event.

The annual report booklet, the size of a popular magazine, was in the packet with a bright red and blue cover picture featuring a smiling grandma hugging a cute little boy. Both were surviving cancer. The grandma in the picture was me! The boy was six-year-old Ryan Michaelis.

AMERICAN CANCER SOCIETY
ANNUAL REPORT 1987
Marvyl Patton and Ryan Michaelis

Many months before, someone from the National Office had called the Minnesota Division office to say they were sending two photographers from New York to take pictures of two cancer patients, a child and a "grandma type." Ryan had rosy cheeks, a new growth of short hair and a charming smile enhanced by his missing front teeth. All day long Ryan and I posed under the photographer's bright warm lights. The picture selected for the cover of the annual report was sealed in a time capsule placed in front of the new national office in Atlanta, Georgia. Someday, when there is a cure for cancer, the time capsule will be opened.

Following the banquet, it was a challenge to get acquainted with as many guests as possible and to find our common experiences. The next day we were feted at luncheon in the Senate Building. I was surprised when Gordy Hoff, who taught my children social studies at Waseca High School, greeted me in his new position as aide to Senator Rudy Boschwitz. Pictures were taken. We called home to tell family and friends when I would be on TV the next day.

Marvyl Patton represented Minnesota at the White House as a part of the National 75th Anniversary celebration. Pictured with Marvyl are Leslie Uggams and Jill Ireland.

The American Cancer Society

S·A·L·U·T·E·S

Marvyl Patton

for her personal courage
in her battle against cancer
and for the hope and inspiration
she gives all Americans in the
fight for life and health.

1988

Ronald Reagan
PRESIDENT OF THE UNITED STATES OF AMERICA

Herman J Eyre, M.D.
PRESIDENT
AMERICAN CANCER SOCIETY

Kathleen Horsch
CHAIRMAN OF THE BOARD
AMERICAN CANCER SOCIETY

We rubbed elbows with the special guests, movie stars Jill Ireland and Charles Bronson, singers Leslie Uggams and Connie Haines, Metropolitan Opera star Marguerite Piazza, and Minnesota's little author, Jason Gaes. At the age of eight, Jason wrote *My Book For Kids With Cansur,* illustrated by his brother, Tim. More pictures were taken of each Courage Award winner with the celebrities.

There was time for sight-seeing. We visited the impressive Viet Nam War Memorial, and the Lincoln, Jefferson, and Washington monuments. Golden daffodils, pink and white tulip trees, and the famous cherry blossoms were spectacular at every turn.

The climax on the last day was going past the throngs of tourists lined up outside the White House fence. We showed our special ID cards and were ushered into the White House Rose Garden, where white seats were set up amidst the cherry trees. Three ranks of TV and news photographers crowded on bleachers in the back. President Ronald Reagan and his wife Nancy walked out of the Oval Office, striding just a few feet from where we were sitting. I considered reaching for his hand to tell him I used to listen to his radio sport casts when he was "Dutch" Reagan in Iowa, but of course I didn't do it.

The President and Nancy mounted the platform set up on the lawn. He spoke, movingly, of the accomplishments we had achieved and honored each one with a Certificate of Courage. The large leather bound certificates bore each individual's name. My award said:

"The American Cancer Society salutes Marvyl Patton for her personal courage in her battle against cancer, and for the hope and inspiration she gives all Americans in the fight for life and health."

Signed: Ronald Reagan,
President of the United States of America.

Hermans J. Eyre, M.D.,
President, American Cancer Society.

Kathleen Horsch, Chairman of the Board,
American Cancer Society.

Nancy Reagan, who recently had had surgery for breast cancer, was surprised by a similar award given to her.

For me, the greatest reward of the event was being one with this courageous group of people who ranged in age from 11 to 82. There was a politician who lost his nose to cancer and had it rebuilt, a coach who was still coaching despite the loss of an arm, a TV personality who lost her tongue and had to learn to speak again, a nun who traveled and lectured in a wheelchair, a teenager who lost her leg but went on to win in Special Olympics. Kindergarten teachers, airline stewards, police officers, housewives, ministers, rabbis, sportsmen, servicemen—together we all were celebrating life after cancer!

~

If you have read this far, it is clear that some of my interests are: children, grandchildren, classical music, nature study, camping and scuba diving. Each patient's unique story will highlight his or her interests. The emphasis I want to give is that continuing with hobbies and interests is vital to quality of life. Don't let disease amputate those interests and joys.

> *Disease will modify the ability to do what we used to do. Instead of regretting that intrusion, be grateful for all the experiences.*

I know some patients who even learned new skills (to speak another language, or to play an instrument). I know a patient who gave two weeks to serve in a foreign country to help build an addition for a hospital in Bolivia. This patient, Bob, had been close to death. In fact, his doctor had advised him to "put his affairs in order." But he did recover. The doctor said he could go on this mission trip. Of course he had limitations on physical exertion during the stay in Bolivia; that's not the important point. The fact is he went, he worked, he built, he helped. What rich memories are his and what rich rewards—so much better than if he had stayed home and been squelched by illness.

Use those experiences and memories now to re-fuel. Life is so much more than cancer. What stands out in life for others to see, for ourselves to see, is what we choose.

Our choice was scuba

I never felt as healthy and free of my disease as I did out of doors. I liked the feel of sun on my skin and the earth beneath my bare feet. From the first moment I entered the underwater world in 1966, it pulled me like an enchantress. In 1974, between the first and second occurrence of cancer, we went diving in the British West Indies. In 1989, Dr. Bowers and Bill's internist both gave the "go-ahead" to resume scuba diving during our vacation.

In the warmth of the Florida sun, we struggled into our heavy rubber suits, designed to keep out the cold of Minnesota waters. Carrying fins and goggles, we climbed into a small boat that smelled slightly oily, as small boats do, and was rather dirty from the travels and debris of river life. As the boat was pushed full throttle, the wind tangled our hair and blew a stinging caress on our cheeks. When we neared the sanctuary, the motor was cut to a low chatter and we crept carefully along toward the fresh water spring. It was not a Minnesota-style spring with a trickle of cold water bubbling up and cascading over rocks. This spring was as big as an auditorium, the water a brighter, clearer blue than the river into which it flowed. Its temperature was cool, but not cold.

I "scooched" my feet into my flippers, put saliva on my mask to keep it from fogging, checked its fit on my face by inhaling until it was snug, and tumbled backwards out of the boat. The thrill of entering a new environment, the privilege of doing so, always filled me with wonder. I sought to gain orientation in the swirling bubbles that accompanied entry into the underwater world.

I scanned the bottom. A large rock appeared on the sand. It was surrounded with green seaweed. I tucked to dive and descended to 15 feet. Stretching out my hand, I touched the large gray rock. It was like soft leather. Slowly it changed shape, raised a head and looked at me. It had long strands of green seaweed dangling from its mouth. It came close and blinked with a small friendly eye. When it blinked, its eyelids didn't close like mine. They were like the lens of a camera, a round circle, which enlarged as the sphincter muscles let it open.

I touched it again, carefully caressing its resilient, leathery skin, which had numerous hairs bristling from it. The creature rolled over on its back, spread its flippers and, like a huge docile puppy dog, it exposed its belly and armpits for me to rub. For a magical moment we exchanged mutual pleasure. Suddenly it pushed to the surface, emitted a distinctive squeak as it inhaled air, and dove again for another mouthful of seaweed.

Its size was like an elephant without legs. Such gentle peaceful creatures, who live a life of slowness and calm in the quiet underwater world. What a privilege it was for me to see, to feel, to enjoy the rare company of the friendly, trusting manatee.

We snorkeled in the bays and canals within walking distance of our campground on Florida's Big Pine Key. We found yellow and pink sponges, purple anemones with translucent waving arms, big, gray loggerhead sponges with numerous deep black vents in their rubbery bodies, small, tightly woven basket sponges that served as pockets for carrying small treasures. On the rocky beaches, there were many dark and checkered nerites showing bleeding baby teeth when we turned them over. In the water were small conchs, called rollers, and large ones with pink interiors and bright blue eyes on long stalks, and pen shells that walked along the bottom, leaning awry like drunken sailors. In the canals, which men had dug for boat access, there were spiny lobsters hiding in every nook and cranny, their long antennae waving curiously. When I tried to grab one with my bare hand, he scooted farther back in his hole and one of his antennae broke off in my hand. I was allergic to eating lobster so I did not try for another.

The next afternoon we went by boat to the reef known as Looe Key. Donning our gear, we held our masks to our faces and stepped off into a fairyland—a forest of white elkhorn coral growing in the deep blue water, white sand on the bottom with large "boulders" covered with soft "moss" in shades of pink and green: living brain coral. Deep purple fronds of gorgonians and delicate yellow and lavender sea fans waved gently in the rhythm of the surf. Graceful schools of fish swam in unison, dressed in exotic luminescent colors. Large flat French angelfish, with fat white lips, were dressed in dove gray with dark polka dots; queen angels with iridescent blue crowns; parrot fish, 2 to 3 feet long, some pink and green, some in shades of blue, and the "stop-and-go-light" one with his red, white and green spots; jacks and snappers in their various uniforms, all with yellow stripes; the sleek and stealthy barracuda hanging just under the surface at the edge of the scene; bright orange squirrel fish with their large dark eyes; red hinds that look like they had measles; striking black and yellow rock beauties and four-eyed butterflies, who try to fool their predators with an eye-shaped black spot near the tail so it appears they are going the other direction; trigger fish, some like dark silhouettes, others like garish beauty queens with black lashes and too much makeup.

That evening and the next morning, Bill found it hard to breathe and he felt dizzy. We walked across the street to an emergency medical center, where they suggested going down to Key West to the decompression center. We knew we had not exceeded the limits of depth and time under water, which can cause compression problems. The doctor told Bill to take off his shirt for an exam. When he saw the large U-shaped scar from lung surgery Bill had about ten years ago, he said it was not safe for Bill ever to breathe air under pressure.

So our scuba days were unexpectedly ended, just as we were about to resume that sport. Both of us felt bad about giving up an activity that had provided such unusual pleasures, but we were glad we could still snorkel. We were very grateful we had not had a serious and potentially fatal accident. We canceled our plans to dive the reef and hoped we might find something interesting close to shore.

In the Keys there was an interesting custom of watching beautiful sunsets—the shifting shades of clouds and sky—pink and blue, lavender and gold, bright orange and vibrant red. As the sun descended in all this glory, the people applauded. In Key West they gathered in the town square, but we heard it up and down the coast and the canals, people alone or together, applauding the glory of the sunset.

What a marvelous way to acknowledge appreciation for God's gifts of beauty. I was reminded of a poem, written by a friend of mine back home. The poem was adopted by our Hospice. I hoped it would be true for me:

"O sun setting,
Filling the world with wonder and beauty
In your dying.
Can
I
Not
Do
the
Same?"

Poem written by jeanette roesler krause
Quoted by permission

Choosing my source

I was tired of "psycho babble." Each profession had a language of words that had special meaning in their context—legal, medical, spiritual, architectural, musical —all specialized groups did it. They used uncommon words or common words to which they gave uncommon meanings. When used in a special setting, it helped with in-group communication in understanding intangible concepts. Transactional analysis identified the child and the adult in each of us as we interacted with each other. Psychoanalysis talked of the ego, the alter-ego and the id. Religions of the Far East and the Native Americans had their gurus and shamans. New Agers had a "child within" or "a little old man" to guide them.

I chose instead to listen to Jesus' parables. He used everyday events to enlighten and make clear. He said we don't need those artificial titles and devices to access the understanding and power of God. We can go direct. We can talk directly to Jesus as our brother, to God as our Father. I resent "new age" concepts, "existential" explanations, "supremacy of self." They are attempts to make us believe we can grasp our own power and self-sufficiency. They may not be "occult" in seeking underworld or Satanic power, but they are denial of God's power.

I struggled to identify the fine line that separates truth from ideology, mystery from mysticism. I believe in the helpfulness of techniques, such as relaxation, memory and imagery, as long as they are true. Those that are contrived, I equate with superstition and false belief.

I believe there are many pathways to God. He reaches mankind in different ways, depending on where we are in our culture, geography and history. Ultimately, He hopes all people will trust him as Father and Creator. Jesus told us to go tell all the world by word and the way we live that God's way is love, and He cares for each of us as an individual of worth (taken from Mark 16:15). Our appeal to Him can be direct. His response to us is direct, although He often uses other people to help us.

Sometimes during my illness God's power seemed elusive. Was it really there, or was it a figment of imagination? Why was it sometimes so clear and at other times so hidden? That was where faith and commitment entered in, where humility, searching and "knocking at the door" became important. Without the surrender of humility, without the need to study, seek and ask, man becomes his own God. There come times of testing in every life where self power is insufficient. Faith is then required to sustain a peace that passes understanding. The evidence of God is strongest then. But it must be sought. The mind and heart must be willing to accept human limits and be willing to perceive and accept a "higher power."

The immensity of God's gift of free will to mankind is overwhelming and indeed it is the source of most of the world's problems.

> *God gave us the choice of how we use our strengths, our ideas and our goods. So many times we do not choose to use them well because we forget to listen to God's directions.*

So many times the burdens of the world, of our day or our work seem too complex. We think we are supposed to control. The obstacles of life are challenges and necessary for our growth, but with God's help and control they are not burdens.

There is so much truth in the statement that giving is more blessed than receiving, but if we live only to give, it is not two-way, and we miss the meaning. We must also have the humility to receive, to give others the gift of our "thank yous."

Reflections on Renewal

When we came home from our extended vacation in 1989, I was reluctant to get back to the demands and responsibilities of committees. I was ready to retire and let someone else do the work. A visiting minister spoke on our first Sunday home. His theme was commitment and dedication, using the unique abilities and experiences given to each one to do something for others. I felt it was being spoken to me. Directly! The choir's response was, "Lord, make my life a window for your light to shine through; And a mirror reflecting your great love to all I meet."[5] [Robert S. Schuler, Used by pemission]

Tears trickled down my cheeks as I realized how close I came to ignoring God's request of me. God's voice was not audible in the usual sense, and probably no one around me heard the message in the same way, but there was no mistaking the impact it had upon me. I prayerfully responded, "Yes, I hear, God, and I will continue. There are workshops to plan, conferences to attend, sick people to visit."

It made such a difference to me when I ceased praying to God to give me help for this or that, and instead began praying, "I love you Father, I trust you. Let me help you by giving happiness to someone today. Please lead me to see at least one joy given to me each and every day, and at least one joy or word of praise or thanks that I can give to someone else."

After all this soul searching, I thought I understood my tasks.

But what happened next? A whole series of medical crises that put me out of activities, kept me homebound for months and sapped my energy. My wheels were taken from me forever, but not pen and paper. Maybe it was time to write!

> Less going—more contemplating.
> Less talking—more listening.
> Less leading—more being led.

Guide-Lines

1. The most important medical Guide-Line: Get the best medical care. The most important God-Line: Be still and worship your God.
2. Do something you've always wanted to do. Enrich your relationships. Renew your lines of pleasure.
3. Be assertive about your care. Ask questions. Ignorance and fear blind you.
4. Borrow strength from others. Give of your strength to others. Asking for help shows you have strength and are taking control.
5. Take responsibility for yourself and your needs. Live, learn and do all you can. Do more than is expected.
6. Set goals and accumulate small successes. Celebrate small joys. Look for treasures.
7. Explore new options, new skills. Let the world in. Let friendships grow. Seek companionship, not isolation.
8. Use your mind to help your body. Knowledge is power. Knowledge dilutes fear.
9. Some things are so important they are worth whatever the cost in fatigue or pain. Allow memories of yesterday to help with today's pain.
10. Spiritual help, Medical help, Self help —All are important in the tapestry of life. Hang on to your lines of hope.
11. Use music, use exercise, use reading to influence your mood and your sense of well being.
12. Write the feelings, the questions and the facts that are important to remember. Write the feelings and the frustrations to get rid of what you want to let go and forget.
13. Control the quality of your life by choosing what you think and do. Smile, say thanks — say I love you to someone.
14. We need the mountain tops to give us vision, but we travel the farthest in the valleys. Accept them, for both are a part of life.

Spiritual help, medical help, self help —
All are important
in the tapestry of life.

Hang on to your lines of hope.

10

Death Threats From Side Effects

August 1989

Small bowel obstruction made us cut short a visit with our son's family. Then last night I had really bad cramps in both thighs. This morning when I got up and was about to wash my face, I was startled looking in the mirror: there were red streaks on my face. It looked as if I had been in a cat fight. There were streaks on my neck, shoulders and legs and lots of reddish-purple dots on my chest and abdomen. I know they were called "petechiae." I looked it up in my home library medical book. Immediate medical care was indicated, so we hurried to the doctor's office without even calling first. The receptionist took one look at me, hustled me into an examination room and called a doctor. Dr. Bowers was out of town. I was immediately wheeled across the street to the hospital. By the time I was in bed, my temperature was over 102, my white count had doubled and my pulse was slow. Diagnosis was thrombocytopenia (low platelet count).

*I discovered how serious it was both from overhearing
doctors' conversations and from articles I requested from the
medical library. Platelets are one of the clotting factors in the
blood, normally measured from 150,000 to 300,000. A count
below 20,000 indicates risk of internal hemorrhage. Below
10,000 often results in brain hemorrhage and death. My
count was only 8,000!*

*First there was a transfusion of six units of packed
platelets and then IV injection of antibiotics. The doctor said
that examination of microscopic slides of my blood showed
many small immature cells. That meant the body was pump-
ing them out, but something was destroying them. The destructive factor might be a virus or a bacteria or a chemical
reaction. They didn't know. There was evidence of internal
bleeding in the bowel and a large hematoma already swelling
behind my knee. I wanted so much to see Dr. Bowers, to have
her guide my treatment, but she was out of town until
Monday. I have so many questions to ask her.*

Dr. Bowers told me on her return that the blood-
thinner coumadin was the culprit. (Coumadin is similar
to warfarin, used as a rodent killer—kills by causing
internal bleeding.) I was taking it as a preventative
measure to avoid the blood clots and embolisms which
also threatened my life. A new CT scan invoked a mild
hive-like reaction caused by the CT dye used, but it
showed no new cancer growth. I was discharged from
the hospital.

A few days later I was home preparing devotions
for a group at church. Somehow I stumbled on verses 2-
4 and 11-12 from Psalm 30 [NIV]. How closely these
verses echoed my situation!

"O Lord, my God, I called to Thee for help
And You healed me.

O Lord, You brought me up from the grave,
You spared me from going down to the pit.

Sing to the Lord, you saints of His
Praise His holy name.

You turned my wailing into dancing;
You removed my sack cloth and clothed me with joy,
That my heart may sing to You and not be silent.
    O Lord, My God, I will give You thanks forever."

For the next six months, we tried to juggle symptoms and medicines to get my body back to near normal. Infections continued to occur one after another. Five times I was in the hospital for a few days. Occasionally I was on morphine, which helped the pain, but I did not like the wooziness, nausea and vomiting that resulted the next day.

In the intervals between illnesses, we took our grandchildren in our "Fifth-Wheeler RV" on several short camping trips to nearby Minnesota State Parks. In May of 1990 we drove our RV to Arizona for a camping trip with my brother and his wife. At the Nature Conservancy park in Ramsey Canyon, Arizona, spectacular displays of 14 different kinds of humming birds filled our days with beauty and delight. In the mountains of New Mexico, far from medical care, I was very sick from small bowel obstructions. In fact, crisis after crisis occurred from 1990 through 1992.

One morning in August of 1990, I awoke and dressed, but the exertion left me breathless. Climbing a flight of stairs, I had to stop midway, panting and resting, reaching the top huffing and puffing. I consulted our resident nurse. She advised me to call my doctor, who ordered hospital lab tests. While I was waiting for results, along came a man with a wheelchair who said, "I'm taking you upstairs to the cancer floor for admission." It was not a false alarm. I had a second pulmonary embolism. I needed complete bed rest and continuous infusion of heparin. I had survived, said the doctor, because I had never smoked, so my heart and lungs were in good condition.

In a couple of hours the danger was over, but this led to a discussion of a living will. I had one on file in Waseca with my doctor, minister and lawyer, but none here in Minneapolis. I was grateful for what had been done so far to prolong my life. But, if at any time I had a crisis that the doctor thought would destroy my capacity to "be myself," I'd prefer not to be resuscitated.

A few days later I was home again. We went to visit our daughter at their motel on Sakatah Bay. I enjoyed the view of the lake and the songs of many birds. We were giving Patti and Greg a brief respite while we "motel sat." As I vacuumed rooms and made beds, breathlessness and pain reappeared. I welcomed Bill's offer to do the vacuuming. There was a tightness across my chest and back and a lump in my throat. It persisted into the evening, so we went to the Waseca Hospital emergency room for evaluation. I had confidence in the staff there, who had helped me through many difficult times. Tests and X-rays showed no ischemia, but the EKG was compatible with lung disease. The doctor said to take it easy until I got home.

Friends invited us to attend the annual Make Today Count picnic the next evening. I was delighted with the work my friend, Eula, had done in reactivating the group, which was defunct for six months after we moved to the retirement community. She and her husband were faithful members. After his death, she felt so strongly about the value of the support group that she got it going again. It took initiative and determination on her part, for there were some who felt the group had outlived its usefulness.

When we came home, the breathlessness was more pronounced, but otherwise I felt OK. It wasn't until a week later that I woke at 6 a.m. with considerable chest pain and irregular heartbeat. I had a tight and heavy feeling mid-sternum and I felt a funny little pulse in my heart. I tried to make a "teletrace call" to check the pacemaker, but it was too early in the morning and the lab was not yet open. I called my doctor and was admitted to the hospital with the diagnosis of a third pulmonary embolism. Statistics said that one out of three are fatal. Lymphoma and all the cancer treatments had altered my veins to predispose to embolisms.

A bird's nest implant

Previously my oncologist and I had discussed implanting a filter to trap clots, but she "shuddered to think of it" because of my increased susceptibility to infection. The vascular tissues and blood flow to the pelvic area had been altered by previous treatment. But after looking at the pros and cons and consulting with other doctors, it seemed to be the only thing to do now. Future embolisms were more of a threat to my life than the filter implant. Doing nothing, the least favorable option, would probably result in sudden death.

An angiogram was done to make sure there were no clots in the saphenous vein or in the area of implant. The filter device came in a long narrow package. Inside the transparent plastic cover were thin little wires stretched about a yard long. At each end of the wires were two tiny little "fish hooks." The hooks attach to the vein to keep the filter securely in place. When released from tension, the thin wires spring back into a tangled mass, something like a tiny Brillo pad. This was called a "bird's nest." Its purpose was to catch blood clots that form in the legs and to keep them from traveling to heart, lungs or brain. Once in, it could not be removed.

There were 17 steps to implanting a bird's nest. The nurse sat at my feet and read the instructions out loud, one by one. I wondered how many this doctor had implanted. A small incision was made in my groin through which the filter was inserted into the saphenous vein and guided into position, just above the bifurcation, where the vein divides to go to the legs.

Hurray! It was quite painless. I went home in a couple of days.

Wow! I was surprised how my moods changed from "I can do anything" to "I can do nothing." On Monday I felt so good, recovered from my pulmonary embolism and bird's nest implant. I was full of energy and had positive thoughts about myself, my world and my place in it. I sang on the way to an American Cancer Society meeting, my first time out after hospitalization. During supper Bill made some comment about my memory loss as perceived by him. I snapped into an angry defensive pit alone. Intellectually I could reason that I was tired, super sensitive right now, needing affirmation but receiving doubts instead. Bill's warm hug and "I love you" an hour or so later helped, but I was still on edge.

During the night I awoke with pelvic pain. Was it the implant? A vaginal infection? Urinary tract infection? I still hurt in the morning, but I got up, had my devotions and went off to an early meeting. The meeting was good, with positive input and positive feedback. It was all downhill from there. I picked up some literature from the American Cancer Society office and went to Southdale Mall to exchange a dress. The stores were not open yet so I sat and read a delightful book while I waited. I went to the bookstore and was frustrated in not finding either of the two books I wanted to buy. I was about to ask them to order, when I realized I needed the restroom. Before I could get there, I had a bowel accident. My good mood was gone.

I felt better the next Monday and helped with I Can Cope class at the hospital. Being part of the group seemed to rejuvenate me. The next evening I got all dressed up to go to the Hennepin County Cancer Society Annual meeting. By the next morning I was bloated, sick, nauseated, weak and depressed. I hurt.

A few days later, my whole leg was hurting from incision to ankle. I detected a blood clot deep in the vein of my calf. I called the doctor and began the routine of using moist hot packs, elevating the leg, wearing thigh high TEDS and resting. I was very uncomfortable with gas passing both up and down, a little bit of nausea and a rotten egg taste in my mouth.

Pelvic pain became more generalized throughout the abdomen, front and back. There was some abdominal swelling and I gained two or three pounds in fluid retention overnight. I called the doctor who implanted the bird's nest. He had never seen this problem with an implant. I consulted Dr. Bowers. Blood tests indicated that my white count was up. I was fighting an infection at the incision site. The nurse found an orthostatic drop in my blood pressure. I must come daily to the chemo clinic for an infusion of antibiotics. Hesitantly I asked my doctor about the short-term memory loss I'd been experiencing. She said it was most likely just the result of all the physical input, part of the protective mechanism of the body to delete short-term memory and keep only what is necessary when the body is under physical stress.

My next journal entry said,

Dear God, what am I doing here AGAIN? In the hospital. I am on IV fluids, nothing by mouth, resting the bowel for 48 hours. I am tired of not feeling good. I hate putting Bill through the worry of repeated hospitalizations. When I am sick I feel so inadequate. I recall how capable I felt and how I enjoyed challenge and accomplishment, but right now, I can't find any of those good feelings.

The next day a parade of doctors came in and out, each making a guess as to what was wrong with me.

"Perforation—ischemia in the bowel—surgery needed."

"Infection—diverticulitis—best handled with medication and diet."

"Disease—do a gallium scan, tag the white cells, but it might show only old lymphoma."

"Disease or infection? Get more stool cultures."

"A chronic condition, results of radiation, radiation proctitis—get a gastrograph—or a colonoscopy."

Send me an angel

I continued in the hospital on IV fluids. I had a lot of pelvic and abdominal pain, both bladder and bowel were unreliable and I wore "Depends" all the time. I tried distraction by turning on the radio. I tried putting cold over the area of pain, then over a collateral area. I tried a hot towel pack. I could not straighten my legs or lie on my back without pain. I had one very brief period of chest tightness and arm pain, perhaps 20 minutes. Positional change lessened the pain some, and it went away before the nurse came. My temperature continued to rise.

Early the next morning I had a phone call from Bill.

"Honey, I won't be in to see you today. But I'm only about forty feet from you."

"What do you mean?" I said, puzzled.

"Well, I passed out last night, found myself on the bathroom floor. I called 911 and came to the hospital by ambulance. I'm in a room directly overhead, two floors up."

After my bath, while the nurse was making up my bed, another nurse came in with a wheelchair and took me upstairs to see Bill. They were checking his heart. He was discharged later that afternoon. Medical conclusion was "syncope of undetermined etiology." Our conclusion was sleepless nights of worry.

Several tests were scheduled for me and I was taken in a wheelchair downstairs for a colon study. I was apprehensive the night before the exam; in fact, I dreamed about it. I saw the monitor in my dream and the small intestine looked like a colander with tiny little round holes all over.

Barium was used for my previous colon studies. The dye used this time was lighter than barium, to detect perforations or weak places where intestinal contents could leak through into the pelvic cavity. After the doctor injected the dye substance into the rectum, a balloon was blown up inside to hold the dye in. I was turned from side to side, my abdomen palpated and viewed from all angles on a fluoroscope. It was a lot more painful than previous studies. Following the test I was taken to a small closet-size restroom to evacuate the dye. I was told not to leave by myself, but to stay there until they came to get me.

After a few minutes, chills began to shake my body so violently that my glasses fell off onto the floor. I had difficulty picking them up. I could not put them back on, so I placed them on a small ledge. I was trembling all over, even my cheeks were shaking so much they hurt. I couldn't stop it! I decided to try to make the shaking movement meaningful. I thought of old camp songs with actions. Even in my discomfort, I thought it was a funny picture, this gray-haired Granny Girl Scout, sitting on the stool, alone in this little restroom, waving arms and singing, "Ah wuni kuni cha." My hands were getting bluish and I continued to shake uncontrollably.

"O God," I prayed, "help me. I can't handle this by myself. Jesus, stand beside me or send me an angel. Please send an angel to touch my shoulder and tell me I'll be all right."

I thought if I pray hard, really concentrated on that heavenly angel, it would help. Who would God send? My mother? No, it would be too hard for her to see me like this. My Dad? Well, he would be calm. Maybe my good friends, Bernadette, or Vivian or Bernice. We'd been close and shared a lot before they died of cancer. Who would God send? I needed help, quickly.

"Please, send me an angel. SEND ME AN AN-GEL!"

Realizing I was in danger of passing out, I yanked the call cord. A nurse came running. She saw my blue lips and the violent shaking. "We've got to get you to bed. I'll call for a gurney," she said, as she pushed me in a wheelchair into the waiting room and rushed off to find a gurney. Nurses at the desk watched me, as did other patients in the room. I began to slide down in my wheelchair, still shaking violently. Quickly, one of the other patients stood up and came to me. He knew me because we had both been volunteers on the cancer floor. He steadied me with a hand on my shoulder. He spoke to me, reassuring words. He stayed with me until I was safe.

Who was he? What was the name of the one sent to comfort me?

It was BILL ANGEL!

A foot-long hot dog

What next? A foot-long hot dog?? Where??? In my leg????

I was sitting on a chair in my hospital bathroom to wash my face and brush my teeth. Suddenly, my left leg began to cramp where it rested on the chair. I stretched it out and pointed my toes toward my knees, thinking to relieve a muscle spasm. I tried to relax it. I stood and leaned against the wall to stretch the calf and thigh muscles. My leg cramped fiercely. I pulled the emergency cord to summon a nurse. She handed me a muscle-relaxing pill. We laughed at my predicament, which made it seem like I was trying to hold up the wall. I laughed at the incomprehensible pain, because I did not think it was life threatening. The nurse helped me back to bed. A gastroenterologist came in. He was being consulted about the adhesions in my intestines. He noted that one leg was larger than the other.

"Six inches larger," said the nurse as she measured my thigh with a tape.

The skin was taut, the leg heavy and difficult to move. An ultrasound of the leg defined the problem. I had a blood clot that extended from my knee to my groin, and probably into the pelvis. The doctor described it as "a foot-long hot dog." My records said I had an EKG, gastrograph, arterial blood gasses, colonoscopy, ultrasound and cultures of stool, blood and urine, but the exact sequence of events was lost in my memory. My temperature soared to 103.6. I became lethargic and unresponsive. My son came to join my husband.

"Are we losing her?" he asked.

Heparin and antibiotics were administered continuously by IV. Bill and Paul left to get a bite to eat. When they returned from supper, they saw a dramatic change. I was sitting up and smiling.

A foot-long blood clot in my left thigh! I had a lot of questions and so did my doctors. I would need monitoring and complete bed rest until the clots were firmly adhered. It would take about a year before they were dissolved; and even then I would have a rough surface on the wall of the vein, making it subject to more clots. Another ultrasound would show when the clot had consolidated and circulation restored. For a couple of months, I would need a continuous infusion of heparin, hospitalization, bed rest. Later, perhaps, nursing home care.

The syndrome of flu-fever-diarrhea that had come about almost every month during the past two years now could be explained as repeated pelvic clots. Areas of ischemia (poor nutrition to the bowel) caused infection and irritation, causing diarrhea. My leg probably would not return to its normal size; with impaired vasculation and drainage, it would always be enlarged. Darn it! That was my "good" leg. The right one had had varicosity's and swelling since college days. Little kids at camp would notice it when I was wearing shorts. "How come you have those big blue bumps on your leg?" they'd ask. But except for cosmetic reasons, I was rarely bothered by the leg, which now moved up a notch in my estimation. It became my "good" leg.

After a time, I was permitted to walk the hospital halls. Pain and heaviness in the now "bad" leg kept me from going any farther than the nurses' station. And even then, I needed someone to hang on to when I walked. What a change from the active "I can do most anything" feeling that I used to think was me.

Facing Changes

I had a lot of thoughts and questions about the changes this last series of events would make in our lifestyle, in longevity, in daily activities. I realized some of those answers would have to evolve and could not be determined immediately. Nevertheless, I felt part of my ability to adjust to changes came from recognizing them, in a sense preparing for them mentally and emotionally. We had already decided that we could not take the trailer and go to Cloud Nine this fall. Bill would have to winterize it and leave it at Dan's for the winter.

Would we have more trailer trips?
Would this be our last Christmas?

How many assaults and complications could my body take?

I was so glad Bill and I talked about those questions with each other. It helped tremendously to acknowledge the doubts rather than hide or deny their presence. Love grew much deeper when we shared both the valleys and the peaks. On my journey, I concentrated on strategies that could help me cope. One rule I learned early was to know as much as possible about my condition.

Stay informed

A doctor substituting for Dr. Bowers came in saying, "We'll start you on coumadin today."

"Are you sure about that?" I said.

"Why, what happens when you're on coumadin?" he asked.

"My platelets are destroyed. Last time they dropped to 8,000."

"When was that?"

"I have had three episodes of thrombocytopenia and it is not considered safe to give me coumadin," I replied.

"I was not aware of that. We'll wait until your regular doctor returns tomorrow."

Once again, I was aware of how important it was for me to know my own history and to be assertive about my own care.

I was glad when the gastroenterologist came in, sat down and gave me his full attention, as if the most important thing for him to do just then was talk with me. I told him how much I appreciated it, that I wished all doctors would do likewise. I wondered if he relayed that message to another "always in a hurry" doctor who came in the next day and actually sat as he talked with me.

"What are we going to do to keep clots under control? Being tied to heparin the rest of your life would be a pain," Dr. Gastroenterologist said.

"Well, that depends on how long is the rest of my life," I replied.

"You should have some good years left!" he said.

"HALLELUJAH!"

The next evening I had the beginning spasms of a small bowel obstruction. X-rays confirmed it. I explained my usual routine for managing them with medication. Of course that medication was not listed on my chart for that admission, and the usual routine was to insert a nasal gastric tube. Bill and I insisted that it could be easily managed, if they would just give me the medication. Without orders, it could not be done that way, so they put down the nasal gastric tube. The pain and spasms continued. Bill left the room. I do not know exactly what transpired, or how he made his point (he said he had to get kind of nasty), but the end result was that I got the medication! The next day Dr. Bowers wrote a standing order for the medication to be given as needed (PRN), at my request.

Getting my PAS port

Many cancer patients have learned to accept the implant of a "port" as routine. Chemotherapy and medications of many kinds can be inserted through the port, go through a catheter directly into the blood stream without a fresh needle poke. Blood samples also can be drawn from the port. It's "nice" because it eliminates the hassle of finding a new site when veins collapse and roll with repeated infusions. The thought of a permanent metallic piece buried under the skin with a plastic tube ending near the heart is a strange and unnerving thought, but one day after seven unsuccessful attempts to get into a vein, Judi brought me a picture of a Peripheral Access System (hence the acronym PAS). Placed in the forearm instead of the chest wall, it was supposedly more aesthetically acceptable to patients. The silicone port, through which the needle was inserted, was the size of a pencil eraser; the whole device about the size of five dimes stacked together. It was a brand new medical device; only six had been used in this hospital. The implant of a port is a minor surgical procedure, so I was considered an acceptable candidate.

On the day surgery was scheduled, Sandie, the wife of our former pastor, called long distance from Kansas City. My lunch was waiting on the tray in front of me as we talked. How fortuitous that she chose that day when I felt the need of reassurance and prayer. Just as we were saying good-bye, the head nurse bustled in and removed not only my uneaten lunch, but everything removable on the window ledge and counters— pictures, flowers, water pitcher—sweeping every flat surface clean. She spread white sheets over all. In response to the question in my eyes, she said the surgeon was coming sooner than expected. This small operation could be done right there in my room. I remember gasping the words, "I hope I have time to catch my breath and get ready." I did not.

Immediately an entourage of people of various skin colors in different colored lab coats paraded in: a hefty black doctor with a green surgical gown and little green cap sitting like a pixie hat on top of his abundant curly hair; a slight Asian doctor wearing a white coat, his dark hair uncovered; a young student nurse wearing a dark blue smock, her blond hair spiked so it stood straight up; my floor nurse in lighter blue. She claimed her role was to hold my hand. The IV nurse wore deep pink and several other medical people from various departments wore color-coded coats. The room was full with this rainbow of approximately ten people. I was reminded of the crazy skits with much nonsense that I've seen at camp programs where an operation with strange instruments is performed on a sheet-clad patient.

"Are you going to stab or cut?" said the pink-and-white nurse.

"Do you want to make the stab?" asked the green-and-black doctor.

Together they covered me with a sheet over my body and another over my arm. Together they ripped a hole in the paper sheet exposing my arm. Pink-and-white nurse poured a large quantity of reddish brown betadine in a large tray and taking a huge sponge swab, she painted my arm. Blue-and-white nurse grabbed my other hand. Green-and-black doctor wanted to reposition the drape and raised my arm, dripping with the reddish colored antiseptic. As I released my held hand, I pulled the drape so I could watch.

"Don't do that," said blue nurse. White-clad patient (me) said, "Can't I watch?"

"Only if you don't breathe on it," said the doctor with the green pixie cap.

As the white-shrouded patient saw her arm dripping with the red fluid, she said, in jest, "Wow, this already looks like pretty bloody surgery."

The green, blue, pink and white-clad medical people began to jest with the patient and each other, relieving the tension with laughter, bantering back and forth about the latest news of bloodless psychic surgery performed by a doctor in the Philippines. He was proven to be a fake who used dead chicken parts, palmed in his hand, to fool patients into thinking he was removing diseased parts from their bodies.

The small PAS port was inserted into a placket created by the doctor's scalpel under the skin. The plastic catheter attached was threaded through the vein all the way to the heart. Pink-clad nurse held in her hand a strange wand-like device that she ran up and down the patient's arm from elbow to shoulder. As she did so, the wand changed color, becoming orange when it was over the vein and indicating how far up the catheter was. When it was satisfactorily in place, a few stitches were taken to draw the flaps of skin to close over the PAS port. Only 45 minutes had passed, and all the rainbow of people filed out. Another half hour passed; my arm began to swell, bleeding under the skin, until it looked like a huge purple tennis ball was implanted there.

For several weeks, it was impossible to find the tiny port with the special needle that is bent at a right angle and aimed to hit the bottom of the port. The only way was to access it under a fluoroscope. I was wheeled to the elevator and taken downstairs to the X-ray department. The doctor and I watched the monitor to see if the needle went into the port.

"Let's inject a little dye to make sure we're really getting through," said the doctor, doing so as he spoke. We could see wisps of the dye fluid going into the vein. I heard the nurses whispering and was alerted. With a shock, I realized the doctor said "dye." I was allergic to radiographic dye, but the doctor had not noticed the red tag on my wrist. Quickly a call was made to my doctor, and the counteracting drugs injected!

Progress!

The enterologist put me on solid food and discontinued the maintenance IV. I was glad to be eating again, but bowel movements were very abnormal. Leakage from the labial veins caused some vaginal bleeding. The clotting time (PTT—which was to become the measure of my safety for a long time to come) was too high, indicating I was getting too much heparin. As my appetite and degree of activity returned, I wrote in my journal: *"I think I am getting better because I'm getting tired of this!"*

Son Dan brought in several videotapes of my grandchildren. I watched and relived the wonder of Eric's birth. The beauty of seeing Dan and Sara with their first baby brought tears to my eyes. The hospital had a good selection of videotapes, too. When I was admitted to the hospital, the only room available was a private one with a VCR. Later when they asked if I wanted to change to a less expensive room I said, "Since I'll only be in a couple of days, I will keep this one." Little did we know that my stay would be a long and critical two months. I had another bowel obstruction. This time we were able to stop it promptly with the medication that was now written into my orders.

From hospital to nursing home

We began preparations for my transfer from hospital to nursing home. Arranging for a wheelchair was easy with a short call to the American Cancer Society. Arranging to enter Colonial Acres Care Center also was uncomplicated, thanks to our decision to live at Covenant Manor with its guaranteed continuing care plan. Five nurses from Colonial Acres came to the hospital to learn the fine points of using the PAS port for continuous heparin infusions. Dr. Bowers ordered heparin to be at the nursing home on my arrival so there would be no dangerous delay.

Activity was to be increased very gradually. The hospital library reprinted for me an excellent article about hematological complications with cancer that "may dominate the clinical picture." Orders for 14 medications went with my records to Colonial Acres. Physical therapy with weights was ordered to maintain strength and to gradually restore use of the thrombotic leg. Also the Aqua K pad (heat pad) was recommended as long as abdominal pain continued. The IV nurse sketched a picture of the PAS port placement to make its access easier. I was warned not to let anyone take blood pressure from that arm, nor was it to be used for blood draw. Either one might damage the catheter.

After a two-months stay in the hospital, I had a great "grand finale" on the last day. To see me and give me hugs and good wishes were Phyllis, Anne, Cheryl and Sharol, Becky, Judy and Judi, Linda, Kathy, Pat, Stan, Jory, Charli, Jerry, Norma, Earl, Melva, and Bill (my angel). Each one was so important to me. I just had to write them down.

About noon, husband Bill took me out of the hospital to Colonial Acres Health Care Center, just across the street from our Covenant Manor apartment. When I entered the hospital the sixth of August, we had no idea it would be cool October when I left.

—And that it would be to enter a nursing home.

Use music, use exercise,
use reading –

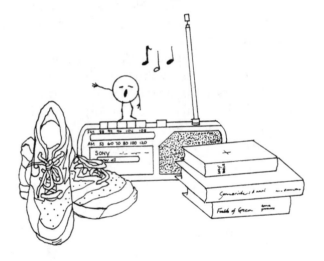

to influence your mood
and your sense of well being.

11

Life in the Nursing Home

What a sight when I entered my room! Balloons, banners, ribbons, pictures, goodies, flowers, streamers, books and a plaque that said, "Each new day is a masterpiece of God." Patti and her little boys had decorated the room so it was beautiful, warm and friendly. Patti had made a huge banner that covered the upper portion of one wall saying, "WELCOME ALMOST HOME." I felt so loved, grateful and blessed with much-loved children, so many friends and my wonderful enduring and endearing husband. As I looked out at the blue sky flecked with white clouds, I thanked God with tears of gratitude.

I ate my first nursing home dinner in bed, ensconced in pretty flowered sheets. (A nice relief from hospital white.) The menu consisted of noodles and stroganoff, lima beans, carrot and raisin salad, and a chocolate sundae that had melted, so I stirred it into my coffee. I enjoyed it all. Flora, a friend from the Manor, was my first visitor, followed soon by Dennis and Bob, a couple of the maintenance men from the Manor. How glad I was to see them and to feel a little closer home. The last night at the hospital I had not slept, so I was tired. That first night in the nursing home I fell asleep instantly with a heat pad on my aching tummy, but warm and comfortable on my egg-crate mattress.

The next day, I had an assessment with the physical therapist. Nurses asked me to help determine my medication schedule. The wheelchair was delivered. I was still in bed for meals. Just as I was finishing my lunch, I caught sight of Henry "tooling" by on his new go-cart. Henry was one of the first residents I met at the Manor; everybody loved him and his attractive relatives who visited frequently. His son accompanied him down the hall as he took his first ride on his motorized cart. When I hailed him, he looked up, surprised to see me. He tried to turn his vehicle into my room. Since he was not used to operating it, there was a good deal of maneuvering and jockeying before getting the cart turned and through my doorway. He made it, with cheers from his son and me. He pushed the forward lever and scooted rapidly ahead, colliding with my bed. My full cup of coffee was sitting on the edge of my tray and went over the edge. I did not think he noticed, so I didn't want to say anything to embarrass him. I was glad to see his familiar face and to have warm conversation with him and his son. After he left, I checked the sheets, expecting they would dry out very soon. Then I checked under the sheets—those little egg cup-shaped pockets were full, each one with its quota of coffee sitting on top of the foam. Later on, when Henry was an expert at driving his cart, we had some good laughs about that incident.

My friends were so thoughtful. Betty brought flowers and candy, and she offered to do my washing. Liz and Roman brought me beautiful ceramic roses. Roman was there with his cancer problems, and many times Liz brightened my day with a treat of homemade caramel corn. Fern brought some of her good homemade pumpkin bread. Dorothy sent a mum plant. When the announcement came over the intercom that communion service was offered in the Commons, I knew I wanted to go to give thanks to God!

About 3 o'clock the next morning, I felt lost when the nurse came in to change the IV and could not get the pump working. The PAS port was irritating and oozing a tiny bit of blood. I felt impatient with the *long* recuperation time this was going to take. I prayed for God's gift of strength, endurance and hope. I repeated from Isaiah 40:31 [NIV], "But those who hope in the Lord will renew their strength. They will soar on wings like eagles; they will run and not grow weary, they will walk and not be faint." Repeating it was not enough. I got out my Bible and read it, letting my eyes and my thoughts wander to seek other reassuring phrases. I prayed that I could continue serving God, follow His leading and let go of self-achievement. In Viktor Frankl's book *Man's Search for Meaning,*[6] he says that having a goal is the key to survival. I thought about that and wrote in my journal:

October 10, 1990

MY GOALS—

Loving each one in my family, individually, with affirmation spoken to them.

Bringing love, gratitude, affirmation and fun to Bill, my so faithful, so loving husband.

Helping cancer patients by revising the manual for the less educated, updating the sexuality videotape, finishing the <u>Mutual Help Facilitators Manual</u>[12]*—all projects I was doing for the American Cancer Society.*

Gradually the daily routine became familiar and I began to feel better. I was awakened at 7 a.m. for a pill; I had time for a lengthy devotions before breakfast. Both the Bible readings and the book Patti left with me helped me find God's presence in this little room—this room in a nursing home. After two months in the hospital, this was progress. Pictures of the family filled the ledges, streamers hung from the ceiling, a grinning jack-o-lantern sat on the floor, cards and flowers were on the window ledge. From the hallway I heard noises of the staff who gave me care.

I now had a regular program of exercises to do three times each day. They were relatively easy, though I could certainly tell that the last couple of months of inactivity had taken a toll on my physical fitness. Still, I felt fairly fit, especially when I was in the physical therapy room and watched the others, some much older than I, most with greater disability. Some had mental disability, too, and others had little hope of improvement. I had realistic hopes of improving and going home. Sometimes I flashed little prayers to God for the man or woman across from me who seemed to be having trouble understanding. Some resisted their exercises no matter how simple they were, some whined, some laughed and chattered inappropriately, some tried hard. I felt a definite affinity with my fellow inmates of a nursing home.

Look, see and hear beauty around you

Frequently, I left the classical music radio station on all night, hoping its beauty would penetrate my unconscious and wake me up with more peace and less resentment. During wakeful dark night hours, the music was soothing, especially if I heard something I had played years ago on a violin in the high school orchestra. Many mornings I heard a vibrant voice singing without words, coming down the hallway outside my door. It was Bob, a stroke patient, who could not speak. When I'd hear him singing, I'd say to myself, "If Bob can greet the morning with joyous voice, I can too." I wonder if he knows he inspired me.

As I was reading my devotions, I noticed the clouds through my window. The sky was blue, but there were big gray clouds and big white clouds swiftly moving. As I watched, a white one came over, closer and lower. It seemed to be coming nearer to protect me from the large dark ones. Then I saw the tops of the trees, only the tops behind the building. Wind was blowing vigorously. I could not see wind, but there was strong evidence that it was there. I took pleasure in seeing the courageous little seedlings growing on the roof top of the adjoining wing. I was sorry when some maintenance person pulled them the next day. Then I noticed a shadow of another tree silhouetted against the building. I could not see that tree at all, but I knew it was there from its shadow on the wall.

I had a sudden insight, a delightful awareness. I was reading a book my daughter gave me, Sue Monk Kidd's book, *When God Whispers*.[7] It sharpened my focus so I could see that God was whispering to me through what I was seeing. I believed, but it helped my unbelief, the part of me that was despairing last night. I wrote in my journal:

October 27, 1990

What a blessing you are to me, my daughter. Several days ago you gave me affirmation of faith in God's working. Did you guess I'd need this book, this reassurance this morning? Probably not, but you gave it to me in advance, so it was there for me when I looked and needed. What a blessing God bonded us together.

Red dots, pink and purple, yellow and green blotches covered my abdomen. The lower pelvis had a deep purple band about two inches high, all due to bleeding caused by the heparin. I was discouraged. I ached all over, even my feet. My blood tests were going down in spite of the injections. Needles did not bother me ordinarily, but now I hated them! I was punctured every hour in my arm or my abdomen. Veins were collapsing, so it was needle sticks and more sticks. The port in my arm was still too swollen to access it. Nothing was working. Nurses tried to explain why it was taking time to reverse the situation and for heparin to be absorbed.

Patience!

New privileges and new challenges

What a relief. By the end of a month I no longer was in a wheelchair and the IV was pulled. No more tubes tethering me. I was learning to give my own injections. I was allowed to shower. While I sat in the chapel for church service, I smelled the fragrance of lotion on my body. I was in my white nightgown with a white shawl on my shoulders, and I felt clean. Clean physically and spiritually. I sang; my voice mingled with some that quavered and others that snored.

After church, I pushed Helen back to her room. She was the widow of a minister, a large woman, very devout and patient. She was telling about the young nurses caring for her, so young and often lacking in sensitivity. "But," she added, "they have not had the years of experience we have, so we cannot expect them to understand." We shared questions about serving God, as limited as we were by age and disease. One young girl in particular was unloading personal problems on Helen. I tried to reassure Helen that she was still serving God with her gift of listening. It occurred to me that perhaps I, too, had been waiting for better health. I'd felt the nudge of God to write. I knew the needs of cancer patients; I now have been given time to write about my faith. I jotted some thoughts in my journal.

November 20, 1990

I wish there were an advocate to speak up for each person who has a soft voice and weak limbs. I notice it especially in the dining room, where some of the staff ignore patient requests. Frequently I do speak up when someone wants soup instead of the main course, or asks for a bib and is not heard.

My table mates eat in silence unless I start the conversation with a thought or a question. I try to think of topics of interest we might have in common, or I ask a question about times before we were in a nursing home. If I start, I am rewarded by their friendly conversation. I am grateful for my place here in "Transitional Care." I hope deterioration does not lead to years of incapacity. I see those who are deformed, palsied, and out of touch with reality. I am glad there are places like Colonial Acres where they can be clean and well fed, but I feel for them in their disability.

I am discouraged by my low blood counts that are not responding to therapy. But I am grateful that I feel well.

I am concerned that Bill does not feel well some days. Is it worry, disease or lack of being in control that makes him feel so terrible? What is best for me to do or say then? I am not responsible for his emotions, yet I do feel guilty about his tension and depression about me.

Patience—and more patience. When I think I have patience, I have to practice more. For example, I feel aggravation when the phlebotomist comes four hours late to draw a 6 a.m. blood sample; when my doctor goes out of town and is unreachable; when meal wait-resses are slow; when I cannot accomplish my goals for the day; when I get behind in writing thank you notes.

I feel gratitude and wonder that I am still alive! With all the major complications, I still function quite well. I can still love my husband, children and grand-children and be support for them. And they still love and support me.

My wheelchair and IV are gone, my pain is less. My bulletin board is covered with cards; friends visit with flowers and things to eat, and they bring their love and good wishes.

Activities? More things are going on than I can possibly do here. A weekly printed schedule, announce-ments over the intercom, and invitations by the staff alert me to choices: watch an old Shirley Temple movie and eat popcorn, help sell white elephants at the bazaar or take my visitors to the dining room for fresh rolls and coffee. I discover that out-going phone calls are still only a dime so I freely call my kids, my husband, cancel out of meetings, order a new book.

Food is plentiful, though not served with the gra-cious flair of our dining room at Covenant Manor. We eat rolls while we wait for bibs and service. With the ringing of a bell, a waiter intones a monotonous hurried grace. Fresh vegetables and fruit are seldom served, but the quantity and type of food must meet rigid state regulations, so a lot of grain and protein foods are served. One table mate came from the dining room for the confused and more disabled. She comments that she does not think this restaurant will last very long. In the other restaurant there was always somebody doing something funny.

When my grandchildren come for a meal, we can eat in the private dining room and read books while we wait. Later we go to the lobby where there are drawers full of games and puzzles.

Physical therapy: for all its importance in regaining or maintaining strength, this is a place where I hear the most groans, not because it hurts (the therapist's job is to make certain it does not), but I think because it reminds us of our limitations, and those restrictions we do not face with pleasure.

After two months in the hospital and two months in the nursing home, I asked for a trial visit home over night. I had not slept at home in our own bed for four months. Good friends were in town and Bill was taking them to the airport early in the morning. Permission was granted. Only later did we discover that Medicare would not pay for holding my nursing home bed that one night. Those few hours to sleep with his woman cost Bill $175.00. What a date!

November 26, 1990

I am home! Sometimes the fact of my cancer seems imaginary, incongruous with my life and present feeling of 'I'm OK.' Hallelujah! Thank you, God, that I am alive! How can I have so many serious complications and near-death experiences and yet bounce back, look good, feel good? It must be due to God and to all those dear loving competent people He has put here with me—my family, friends and medically-knowledgeable people. Each day I try to remember that. Do I share it enough? I don't want to drive people away with piety. It seems easier for me to live by God than to talk of God. Should I let more words of praise to God punctuate my conversations?

It is hard to believe I was so ill that I needed four months of hospital and nursing home care. I like to think of myself as

*resilient and healthy, but more and more parts of me are
faltering. (Not failing, though without medical interventions, I guess my body would have quit breathing and beating
some time ago.)*

Back in the hospital

A new problem scared me and required new medication to prevent a stroke. In addition, a particularly
severe intestinal obstruction with a lot of vomiting and
pain lasted for three days and put me back in the hospital. It almost led to risky surgery. The surgeon came
with Dr. Bowers to discuss this possibility. They suspected a bowel perforation. The seriousness of the situation escaped me until after the crisis. The doctors
asked if I had passed any gas. Under morphine's influence I blithely replied, "Yes, I've been tooting all morning." I had the sensation that Dr. Bowers clapped her
hands and danced on my bed in relief.

A cancer patient friend was in the room next to me.
We knocked a friendly code on the wall separating us.
Support came, too, from the ward secretary, who gave
me a small corsage, and from the other staff friends,
who visited with love when they were off duty. If I had
to be hospitalized, those friends made it a pleasant
place to recover.

Then one evening, Bill and I went down the hospice wing of the hospital to look at the art work. There
was an ever-changing display on the walls, works of
different artists as well as patients. Previously when I
walked down that corridor, my thoughts had been about
how comfortable and attractive the area was. Wallpaper, bedspreads and curtains were coordinated with a
theme: Western, Scandinavian or Elizabethan. Each
room had a hideabed for a relative to stay overnight.
Usually it was a wonderful comforting feeling to know

that such care existed. I was surprised at my reaction this time: "No, I do not want to be in here! Let me go home."

During the entire week before I left for home, my roommate had the bed by the window and wanted the blinds drawn so I did not see outside as spring changed the drab brown color of winter. As we drove from under the canopy of the hospital on the day of my discharge, I was stunned by the verdant, vibrant green of the bushes, trees and grass. It was as if God had turned on a spotlight. Powerfully in my mind the Lord's message came to me: "I am giving the world back to you, my child!"

Write the feelings,
the questions and the facts
that are important to remember.

Write the feelings
and the frustrations
to get rid of what you want to
let go and forget.

12

Where is Joy?

Bill took a friend of ours for a cancer check-up. He was told to come back for a recheck in two years! Of course I was glad for him, but there was some small part of me that said, "How come?" I've had to go in every month for the last eight years. In fact, over the last 20 years the longest reprieve I ever had was six months. I didn't want so many problems! I'd like to be free to travel like some of our friends—across country—over seas—on cruises. A little part of me is envious and angry.

I have learned, though, that if I accept what is, see the privileges, the opportunities and the blessings of family and of faith, I have no anger and no envy left, just some sadness for what I cannot do. God has given me a special place in His world, with special lessons to learn, and special service to give. "It's only when I compare my lot in life with that of others that the destructive emotion of self-pity is allowed to engulf me," says one of my devotional readings. "If I will do what I am given to do, I will be content."[8]

The serious business of heaven is "JOY," says C.S. Lewis in his *Letters to Malcolm Chiefly on Prayer*.[9] I like that! Why can't I shed my pain, just let it drop from my body and feel JOY? A week or so ago when the pain of small bowel obstruction and infection seemed rampant in all of me, Bill gave me a hypo. It was like a gentle wave of the ocean that washed the pain away. I felt it leave. It was such a relief. But the next step was oblivion, as the medication induced sleep.

I think of the unbounded joy of my grandchildren. Delight in everything permeates their presence and brings joy in just observing them. No wonder Jesus said we must enter the kingdom of heaven as little children. My mind travels on thinking of each grandchild and the special gifts they are. Each one so precious, so individual and unique in their ways and in their gifts to me—intangible gifts of person, of love, of dependency, of creativity, of appreciation, of enthusiasm, of quietness, of exploration, of discovery, of activity and of energy! I wish I could recapture any of those traits, just to feel purpose and delight in my being. As I wrote those words, my husband came to me, gave me a kiss and told me he delighted in my being. Heavenly Father, I thank you for him.

The other night my best friend, Dena, asked how I was feeling. I was surprised at the vehemence of my reply. When people ask how I am, usually I say "good" because I don't like to be a complainer. With Dena, however, I told her how tired I was of hurting and having health problems. For the last six weeks I have been hurting. The CT scan shows two new problems: a cyst on the right ovary and calcification of the appendix. To combat infection I am on a nasty medicine that causes severe headaches and tingling hands, so I'm on another medication to counteract that. I'm sure I sounded angry and discouraged. She listened and said little in reply. We went to the theater and laughed together at the play we were seeing.

After the play, Bill and I drove the 80 miles home in hard-driving rain. We didn't talk much. I thought a lot. Was it good that I spouted off so heatedly. I suppose so. Now could I let go of all negative thoughts and heal? I've told other people that our minds are like computers —we put in negative thoughts and that's what comes out. We must put in some positive thoughts, some joyful thoughts from self or from others if we want to find joy.

While I've been writing this book, I've gone back over notes written years ago. Day before yesterday I threw some notes in the waste basket. They embarrassed me and I decided not to use them. I changed my mind the next morning and tried to retrieve them, but the trash had already been taken out. What I had written back in 1977 was a catalogue description of symptoms I was having, each followed by a possible diagnosis with a question mark. The reason I decided to include them is because many, probably most of us cancer patients, go through "fear phases" when every little "owie" triggers the question, "Is it cancer?" Most of the time it isn't. Life goes on and we forget about it. That's why I felt embarrassed and trashed the notes.

Recalling the reality that such fears are almost inevitable following a cancer diagnosis, I reconsidered and thought I'd write about it. Almost all of us go through those phases, even though hypochondria has not been part of our lives. We have choices: we can choose to hang on to those fears and let them continue to worry us, or we can get so busy living that whatever it is that hurts becomes a minor inconvenience.

Surviving a doctor's insensivity

I was back in the hospital again—two new problems, never there before. Were they serious? Would it mean surgery? Would I recover? Would it always hurt?

Did I dare let go of the hurt, pretend it's not there? If I
didn't tell anyone, would it go away? How simplistic to
think I might cure myself with happy thoughts. Or was
it?

Judi, my nurse, asked me, "Is there such a thing as
learning survival skills and strategies? All of those serious crises you've had would have tipped many people
over the edge—they would have died. You're obviously very much alive. Are there adjustments and accom-
modations and survival skills that can be practiced and
learned?"

"I think so."

I wondered about the doctor on call. Did he feel
compassion only for the patients who were dying, but
not for those of us who were living on with problems?
When Dr. Bowers was out of town, the doctor on call
said to me one day, "I don't see why you need to stay in
the hospital. You might as well go home. It's a nice day
out. You can stay if you wish and see Dr. Bowers tomorrow, but there is no reason you need to stay. The tests
are all OK."

I had been asking for two days for the results of the
blood tests, but the nurses were too busy to check and
tell me. So I asked "Dr. Oncall" for the results. He read
off the name of the tests done but gave me no results. I
asked specifically for my white count. It was twice as
high as my normal count. The number he gave me
signified an infection in my body, so I asked for his
medical opinion about my current problem and intense
pain.

His "parent to child" reply was,

"Whatever makes you think you have infection?
The white cells are all of the right kind; there is no shift
to the left. You know we doctors can tell those things.
You have no fever, the neurologist says you are all
right, the gynecologist says you are all right. Now you
may have pain—I believe you have pain, you probably

have a lot of adhesions. The way radiation was given 20 years ago, that was sometimes a problem but not so much today. Now listen to me!" He pointed his shaking finger at me, "Are you listening? You just have to learn to live with pain!"

The never-ending search for answers and guidance

Home again. On a cold gray, wet morning I had my devotional time on the deck. I liked to read and think and pray at tree top level, where I could look at sky and clouds. I read Psalm 31 in Leslie Brandt's book, *Psalms Now*.[10] Then I read the same Psalm in the Revised Standard, King James, New International and the Living Bible. Some words jumped out at me:

"I will be glad and rejoice in thy mercy; for Thou hast considered my trouble; Thou hast known my soul in adversities; And hast not shut me up into the hand of the enemy; Thou hast set my feet in a large room. Have mercy upon me, O Lord, for I am in trouble; mine eye is consumed with grief, yea, my soul and my belly!" [KJV]

Yes, my belly! And my back, my neck and my head. When I was hurting, it was hard not to take inventory of the places it hurt. It was hard to let go of feelings of pain and concern and just show happiness. The "fruit of the spirit is joy," it says in Galatians 5:22, but sometimes it's hard to radiate joy.

The morning's devotions gave me directions. I was reading in James when the wind blew the pages open to Hebrews 12:12, so I began reading there. I most certainly am surrounded by many faithful ones. I don't suffer criticism or sweat blood in agony from my enemies. I must lift my aching arms, stand strong on my weak knees that others who came after me may not falter, but find encouragement (my interpretation).

Maybe it is not intended for joy to be felt at all times. There are times to develop endurance and patience. Maybe I need not feel guilty that I couldn't find joy; perhaps that day's lesson was faithfulness or thankfulness.

There was a knock on the door. Jim, my neighbor, presented me with a pan of fresh picked, bright red strawberries. I could celebrate that with joy. The phone rang. It was Jeanne. Her husband Bill (from my angel story) died two weeks ago. His funeral was a celebration of his life, not a dirge for his loss to us. Jeanne has multiple sclerosis with significant limitations, yet today, she was helping me find solutions to my distress. I could celebrate that with joy.

Stay tuned into nature and listen to God

Our trailer was parked at our son Dan's home in the country near Watkins, Minnesota. Bill remained asleep as I crawled out of bed, brushed my teeth, washed my face, took my before-meal meds, counted out the six other pills for after breakfast and gave myself the heparin shot in the thigh. I made a cup of instant coffee and heated a Poptart in the microwave. Picking up my Bible, I sat on the couch where I could look outdoors. I felt the soft brush of a gentle breeze across my arms, legs and face. The migrating birds had returned. I saw the cinnamon flash of the brown thrasher and heard his repetitive mimicking song. I saw the white flick of the flicker's rump feathers, heard a plaintive phoebe, the "dee-dee-dee" of a chickadee. Gold finches were taking their roller-coaster flight with a "per-chic-ory" call. Sparrows and robins, too, came across my stage, which was set with a backdrop of young, light green maple leaves, a bank of red and yellow tulips next to the house and a host of golden dandelions at the edge of the yard.

I began my devotions by reading favorite passages from Isaiah and Romans. On the back cover, Bill had written down some of his favorite passages. One by one, I turned and read the passages he had underlined. How blessed I was to have my husband, one whose faith complimented and enhanced mine. On the Mother's Day card he gave me, he quoted from and added to Reverend Nelson's sermon: The ingredients of a good marriage are Commitment, Communication, Certainty, Christ, and Bill added Children. Without Bill's love and constant care, not only would I not celebrate Mother's Day, but I probably would have lost my life to the complications of cancer long ago. Thank you, God, for my husband.

As these thoughts of gratitude surfaced and paraded before my consciousness, I wrote them in my journal. I thought about our table conversation a couple of nights ago. We had talked about the wonders of electronics, cordless telephones that enabled us to hear another's voice spoken way across the country. We could hear it only with the right equipment, finely tuned to pick up those waves. The waves were there all the time, but we must be tuned in.

Why should we question or doubt that we could hear and understand the voice of God. The tuning was even more miraculous, both more complex and more simple. We needed only ourselves; the equipment and sensitivity were built into us. To hear, we did not need to understand the mechanics; we needed only to believe and to listen. The belief came first. When I believed God spoke, I heard him everywhere. Staying tuned in to God's wavelength kept me from being discouraged or despondent with the repetitive complications and annoying side effects of cancer. If I concentrated on what He was saying to me and showing me, I was overwhelmed with gratitude and wonder.

I reread the thoughts in my journal when we got home. That was all true. Still there were days when I did feel weary and burdened with the weight and the complications.

May the words of my mouth . . .

A funny pop, a pang of pain, came as I leaned over the grocery cart to reach an errant can of fruit to put it on the check-out counter. A week later, I visited a friend in the nursing home. I give her a hug.

"That feels so good," she said. "I miss the conversation and the people we used to have dinner with. I miss their hugs."

"Well, I have lots more. Here's another one for you," I said. She reached for me eagerly and gave a heartfelt squeeze. Another rib popped. Not long after, I was lying on the beach with my infant grandson and my daughter. We watched her older boys running in and out of the water. We were having our usual good mother-daughter exchange of ideas and appreciation of little boys. I did not even shift my position when I heard a quiet pop, with a distinctive twinge in the rib section. The fourth rib broke when I was sitting at the lunch table with Dena admiring the woods next to the Covenant Manor dining room. Dena and I have been friends since high school days. She saw a strange expression cross my face and asked if I was all right. I had just felt and heard another funny pop.

Four broken ribs; each one took a couple of weeks to heal. It hurt when I turned over in bed. It hurt when I tried to run the vacuum cleaner, when I scrubbed, when I bent to pick something up from the floor, or when I stooped to help the grandchildren. It also hurt to sit still. Did bending and lifting cause new ones to break? Was it symptomatic of my lymphoma?

In the midst of my worries, God gave me the strength to minister to others. My chaplain asked me to visit a newly-diagnosed cancer patient who was turning inward in despair and confusion. We agreed to meet. I swept the porch to get ready, hoping we might talk out there. He came early. It was chilly outside, so we sat inside at the dining room table with fresh coffee and hot muffins. He had a buoyant personality. He was responsive; he even took notes. I tried to be aware of listening enough and not talking too much, but after he left, I wondered if I said what was right for him. Talking to him helped me forget my pain, but had I helped him? Because of his early arrival, I had not had time for my devotional reading. When I opened my Bible, I was answered! I read in Exodus 4:12 [KJV]: "Now therefore go, and I will be with thy mouth and teach thee what thou shalt say." And in John 17:8 [KJV], "For I have given unto them the words which Thou gavest me, and they received them and have known surely that I came out from Thee and they have believed that Thou didst send me."

I could hardly believe what I was reading—out of the whole Bible, those were the very verses I needed. How did God know? How did He hear me and answer my questions?

In a pit

Most mornings I woke up discouraged by my pain, not liking my situation. I had to open the curtains, thank God, read devotions and interact with people before I began to feel OK. I wanted to sing praises and really feel it, but I was having trouble. I had been in the hospital five times that year. I was having pain, day and night. I wanted so much to feel grateful, joyful and responsible, but what I felt was OW!

I made an appointment to see a neurologist. We hoped he had some medical answers and cures for all the pain. All kinds of bizarre explanations ran through my mind, from chronic pelvic infection to tumors on the spine. Was the medication destroying my bones? Did osteoporosis hurt? I had little energy. I was not me. What was I to learn from this? What didn't I understand that God was trying to teach me? Was this God given? I didn't believe it was, but I knew He could help me with it, help me grow, learn, be more responsive to Him and more helpful to others, with it, in spite of it, or because of it. But I just felt miserable. I couldn't even attend the funeral of my good friend Hazel. I wanted to be there for her family. I wanted to be there for myself, to feel the bonding and the sharing of my friends who would be there.

I was in a pit and couldn't climb out. How long would this go on? What could I do? I had trouble feeling God's nearness and His direction. All I could do was endure and take one step at a time.

Why did I hurt so much? There had been no real "highs" lately, time when, inexplicably, I'd find the right verse, or hear the right words to feel God was close to me. My daily devotions were small Band-Aids of reassurance, but they did not give surcease of pain. Where could I find it? I was so tired of working for cancer control. That I could hurt so much and feel so inadequate was strange. It seemed that all I did was take my pain pills and sleep. It was hard to reconcile that this was me. Could I rise above it with determination? Or should I give in to it and recognize that I needed rest?

My body hurt. It yelled, "don't touch." It screamed, "let me alone." I tried to ignore it. It hurt too much to be ignored. Pain got in the way of whatever I wanted to do, even doing something simple like tying my shoes or eating my breakfast.

What was going on inside my body? I tried to let go and not think about it. I tried to research and understand it. I tried to preoccupy myself with people, plants, music and books. They were good temporary modifiers, but imperfect masks that couldn't hide all the hurts.

After my appointment, the neurologist's secretary called with good news and bad news. A CT scan of the spine showed no cancer there—certainly good news. It did show advanced degeneration of the spine, stenosis of the spinal canal, displacement of two vertebrae—bad news. Lumbar vertebrae #4 and #5 had shifted out of alignment. My pelvis had been thrust forward. I learned a new word for my vocabulary: spondylolithesis. I supposed it was of little importance, but I also lost three inches. Accordion-like pleats appeared in my flesh, and I lost my belly button in the folds.

The next six days I was in the hospital. Pain meds were increased; they made my head and my stomach hurt. I didn't feel like writing in my journal, but I read a book of poetry written by other cancer patients and then I wrote my own poem:

PAIN

Who are you? Why are you here?
You've been with me off and on over the years,
But now, have you moved in permanently?
Go Away! I don't like you!
I want to let you go, but I feel I must keep track of you—
Pin you down, so the authorities can see your face.

You are a hoodlum, sneakily hiding
In the recesses and tunnels of my lower regions.
We keep trying to catch you and learn your name.
We pick up other little villains.
We look them in the face, but they are not you.
Why do you taunt me with pain?

You throw sticks and stones and sludge and glue,
Which obstruct the streams and rivulets
That should flow smoothly in my body.
Are you the leader of a gang,
Capable of some dastardly explosive deed
That will again threaten my life?

I try to muster my body's policemen,
Those white cells, designed to control and capture you.
They can't find enough helpers to surround you
And render you impotent.
They can't even work up enough heat to threaten you.
My bones and cells are tired.

Do you have long nails
Crawling inside my tunnels, irritating and scratching,
Hiding in those twists and turns so we cannot find you?
Are you finding secret places
From which you shoot out poison darts
That cause unyielding pain?

I call on my God and my doctors
With their help I am learning endurance and patience.
Is there a purpose for your continually pestering me?
Are you trying to tell us something?
Are you more than an annoyance
Continuing to occupy me?

It's not just that small area you occupy though,
You furrow my face with pain lines instead of smile lines.
You cause intestinal contents to heave from my mouth.
You minimize my joy!.
I cannot pick up that cherubic smiling grandchild.
I cannot roll over to embrace my love.

I cannot think clearly with your presence!
(Or do I think more compassionately for others?)
It does help to ignore you, to search for service I can give.
I can find pleasures everywhere,
And for these I am thankful!—But I am also wishful.
Pain, I wish you'd go away!

© Marvyl Patton

August 5, 1991

It's 7:30 in the morning, and I'm home with a new TENS unit and more pain medication. I ease myself out of bed so the hurting doesn't make me groan or collapse. In the bathroom I sort out my "not with food" pill and the pain pill. After taking them I gratefully ease back in bed, gingerly, because it hurts to go from one position to another. I'm glad I don't have to get up yet; I can rest in oblivion for a couple more hours.

10:30—I hesitate to move, but it's time to get up. That means pain and pills, a needle full of heparin in my bruised arms, electrodes on my back and turning up the 'pain zapper.' I long to bound out of bed, put on a minimum of clothing and go outside to start a day full of fun. This seems like a lot of effort with a minimum of return. It stifles enthusiasm. Am I sorry for myself? Yes, kind of, I guess, though I don't like that label.

I went on the deck to eat my breakfast and read my daily devotions. I must focus on beauty—the magnificence of the hibiscus blossoms, the cheeriness of the pink and purple vincas, marvel at the cottonwood tree that is voluntarily growing in a pot. And thank God for the love and care my husband gives. Thank husband too! Thank God for the husky baby boy He's given to my daughter and her husband and rejoice that I am able to go the 60 miles to be in church for his dedication.

My morning devotions always help. Today's message is to give to others and to love others. That's especially true now. When I concentrate on self, take assessment of how I feel today, it's no good. The way I find good and fulfillment is to concentrate on others. Forget self and physical questions and try to give others a listening ear, a reaching out in friendship.

I really enjoyed getting lost in a new friendship today. A new patient and I shared experiences and feelings amazingly alike. We sat in a restaurant, drinking coffee. I lost all track of time and was late getting home. Bill became anxious about my health and whereabouts. His overbearing concern dampened my joy and made me wonder about my judgment.

I do wonder about my value—the medical bills and the worries my family endures. Is it part of God's plan for our mutual learning and caring? The stresses are great. Once in awhile that is OK—but repeated and repeated and repeated?

Am I magnifying my ills and my confusion? My husband and my doctor say I am not. They say I handle my restrictions and adjustments amazingly well and that I tend to minimize my problems.

I'll pull myself up and out of my funk. I've done it before. I know how. I just wish I didn't have to, that I didn't go down to a low ebb of endurance minus joy. Joy should be spontaneous, not something I have to work so hard to find. Not something qualified with "yes, buts." Dear God, it is hard to be human, subject to human aches and ills and self doubts.

Doin' in our Doin' Buggy

My mind and body made adjustments with pills and a new TENS unit for pain. Weeds took over my garden, but I became more comfortable. Tentatively, we considered whether we could travel with our trailer. As my bones continued to become more fragile and brittle, I could expect more rib fractures, the results of cancer, radiation and heparin. And old age, too. Keeping active would help slow degeneration. We planned a short and easy trip to "try me out."

Traveling up the North Shore of Lake Superior, it was fun to see our old camping grounds at Gooseberry Falls and Split Rock Lighthouse. We stopped at the little General Store in Shroeder to select apple sausage from the 35 kinds they had on display. We parked our "Doin' Buggy" (that's what we called our trailer) at a campsite called "Happy Land." It was pleasant to sit under the birches and balsams with a cup of hot coffee or a glass of cold juice. We sat on a rock and watched energetic young children scamper in and out of the cold water.

Thunder Bay and Grand Portage National Monument did not exist when we were up here many years ago. We visited historic Fort William and learned history from the costumed guides. We sat on a park bench to admire Kakabeka Falls. We explored the open amethyst mines and picked up samples, paying for the sackful by weight. We took a short boat cruise down the Kaministikewia River. Our truck bounced and rumbled over the railroad tracks as we explored the yards where ships and railroad connected with their loads of iron ore and grain.

I wore my "pain zapper" most of the time and we both felt very lucky that we could travel again after the medically-eventful year. I came fortified with a progressive scale of medications to interrupt pain and prevent problems. Also my implanted pacemaker with a teletrace unit to check its function, the TENS unit, thigh-high anti-embolism stockings (known as TEDS) and adult diapers (known as Depends). I wished I were still the free-spirited traveler I once was.

Each day, it was more painful to walk. On day five, we found a clinic for my weekly blood tests, a cancer hospital, then a doctor to seek help for pain. He prescribed a stronger medication. It was not effective and even the TENS unit brought no relief.

My journal said:

The pain in my back and pelvis is close to excruciating. It sure hampers my stamina and sense of fun. I am exhausted from hurting.

Back in Duluth, I sat in the truck, warmed by the sun, trying to read, while Bill climbed the stairs to tour the ore boat William A. Irvin. I had always wanted to see the flight of hundreds of hawks during migration, so we drove to Hawk Ridge on the Skyline Drive. We spent an hour watching and talking with the Audubon bird counter. The hawks were not flying; we saw only three.

When we returned home, I was admitted to the hospital again. X-rays showed two compression fractures in the spine, no doubt caused by Thunder Bay's bumpy railroad tracks.

Hell on earth!

Hell in my life! I experienced it. It took my speech, my mind, my body, my muscles, my nerves, even my spirit.

Medications were infused into my body by mouth and by injection following the diagnosis of two compression fractures of the spine. I felt a strange mix of awareness and confusion. I could not write in my journal. I lay in my hospital bed in pain, but Paul's words to the Philippians (4:8) kept recurring to me: "Think on those things that are pure, are holy, are lovely," so I looked at the white sheets covering four inches of foam that cradled my spine.

A new chaplain came in to talk with me. During lucid times, we had good conversation. But pain still encompassed me. More medication. More confusion: I wanted the bread left on my tray to be saved for the lady with the dog, so I pushed it into a baggie. My husband tried to tell me there was no lady, no dog. I insisted there was. A nurse from the "pain team" came in for assessment and said to try another medication. My daughter visited and left in tears, because I was trying to play backgammon on the squares of my hospital gown. More pain. More medication. I thought I heard my father calling for help, so I jumped out of bed and ran out into the hall. Then, I was tied down by restraints.

A fentanyl patch was put on my back. Over the next 72 hours it would release a continual dose of medication. The next morning, I awoke pain free. Euphoric. The nurse untied the restraints and I got out of bed to go to the bathroom. OOPS, blurry vision, nausea, vomiting. Then, I had a strange feeling of "prickly green things" on my feet, moving up my legs, covering my whole body. I began to sneeze, cough and twitch. Quickly, the nurse whisked off the pain patch and injected a counteracting drug. Muscles and nerves stretched, contracted violently, making my arms and legs jerk into the air. I could hardly breathe. Deep body wrenching spasms overwhelmed me. A doctor was consulted and I was wheeled, bed and all, out of my room, down to the anesthesia recovery room, where vital signs could be monitored constantly.

"What's this twitching and jerking?" asked the doctor. I thought that was a dumb question, but I couldn't answer. More counteracting drugs were injected, which led to more violent spasms and convulsions. Mind and body were gone: the pain and anguish of Hell.

The doctor told my husband that he was injecting an amnesia drug so I would not remember it all. When Dr. Bowers came and held my hand, I ceased struggling and fell into a deep sleep. I have no recollection of what transpired next.

In other times of crisis I was always able to pray, was able to feel the "everlasting arms" of support from God. Had I had false hopes in a false faith? Nothing was left, nothing but fear, doubt and cynicism. I felt forsaken and shattered.

I listened to my pastors who came to call. They still had faith. I listened to fine music of the masters who 200-300 years ago wrote inspired compositions to honor God. How had that lasted so long if it were not true? My husband still believed. So did my friends at Covenant Manor and my friends at Trinity Church. What had happened to me and my faith?

I pondered. Here I was in a clean bed, in a clean hospital, surrounded by high tech and skilled people to help with my illness, and yet I had to struggle to keep my mind on anything pure, lovely and good. Was there something I was supposed to learn from that horrible experience? What would I have done in lesser circumstances? What if I lived in a third world country, dirty, poor, hungry and hurting, with little hope. Then, what if along came a kindly person who saw me, really heard me and who told me about a man who taught us how to live with pain, who promised peace and comfort, if I'd just believe and live in a loving way. What tremendous power there was in the caring and helping of someone like Mother Theresa, who showed love and listened to the poor and powerless. We who know the power of God's love have little comprehension of the power of that love when some downtrodden person hears about it for the first time. No wonder they got excited.

I understood as never before about missionaries and their people, about their excitement and commitment. That was something that had always puzzled me and left me a bit in awe. Missionaries in foreign fields saw excitement in people who heard the message of Jesus' life. We heard it all the time and we didn't get overwhelmingly excited. My great-grandfather was a missionary who came to the United States from Germany. In junior high, I had thought I'd like to be a missionary and carry Christianity to some foreign people.

Now, I was struggling with cynicism. Had I been worshipping a faithless God? I felt I had nothing left.

On the day I realized my faith was gone, others kept the faith. I was at my weakest, totally lost, but others were still believing, trusting, praying and singing. Because they believed, could I believe again? The fellowship that had developed through the years did sustain me and overcame feelings of doubt and cynicism.

Other people's caring, believing and praying did guide me, even though they were unaware of it. The glory of God was shining through others.

*Control the quality of your life
by choosing what you think and do.*

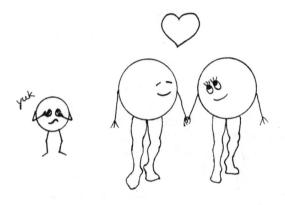

*Smile, say thanks —
say "I need you."
Say "I love you" to someone.*

13

Healthy Parts of Me

Suspended time.

Everything on hold.

That's what happens during a big snowstorm in Minnesota, when everything stops waiting for abatement. Pain was my snowstorm. How long would it last? What would I discover in the aftermath? If I dared to move, an agony of pain went in a semi-circle around my back.

An orthotist brought in two braces for supporting my back. Neither of them fit. Next, he asked me to put on a T-shirt, while he wrapped yards of gauze and wet plaster of Paris around my body, from neck to pubic bone. After it dried, he slit it open, sprung it apart to take it off, then used it as a mold for a custom-fitted brace. He brought it in a day later, heavy white plastic to cover me from collarbone to hips, fastened with velcro straps in the back, a large cut out in the front for my breasts. (Was it X-rated?) Arms and legs protruded from it like a turtle. When my grandchildren came to visit in Halloween costume, I explained that it was my Mutant Ninja Turtle disguise.

As I looked back, I found the whole experience interesting from both a personal and professional perspective. Many times, I have been both observer and participant, both patient and healer, both intellectually aware and psychologically vulnerable. I have a tremendous need to understand and control whatever I can, rather than being submissive to the onslaughts of this disease.

Perhaps the way I clung to my little blue journal book was a slightly humorous sign of that need to control. I wanted to clutch it even under anesthesia. There is no doubt in my mind that it represented both a conscious and an unconscious effort to maintain a segment of control and identity. My nurse asked if I was embarrassed by the happenings of that week. I supposed she meant being tied in bed, talking nonsense and the other non-cognitive things I did. No, not embarrassed at all, because I was not in control. The drugs controlled my mind and muscle. Nor was I angry with my caregivers for the medications given to me. They were sincerely trying to give care. What I did object to were their long serious faces, of which I was aware.

Who is this woman?

When I went home, the American Cancer Society supplied a hospital bed. It had side rails, by which I could gingerly pull myself to turn, and controls so I could change my orientation, up and down. Four inches of foam on top of the mattress supported my body, around which was the brace to protect my spine. The brace was to be worn day and night.

It seemed unreal to me that I was just vegetating. I'd always been active physically and mentally, seeing many interesting things in which to become involved, choosing my path and realizing the results of the choices I made. This episode took so much out of my hands. Even thinking over the awards I had won seemed to belong to the life of some other woman. It was strange, very strange, this separation I felt from the me I'd always known. Sharing retirement years with Bill was not supposed to find me inadequate, unable to do for myself even very simple everyday things. He washed clothes, did dishes, cleaned the kitchen. The plants needed watering and debugging, but I could not get the stuff from under the kitchen sink, nor carry a full pitcher of water. We talked about loss of self, loss of my role in life. There had been some gradual changes, but now it seemed so total. Loss of ability to even lie down in my own bed with my head on Bill's shoulder. I felt empty when he stood over my hospital bed in the living room to kiss me good night, and then went alone into our bedroom.

Was this temporary? As weeks and months went by and new physical problems cropped up, I was less and less sure that I'd get back to "me." That was sad.

Did my family ever wish we'd get it over with? They went up and down, up and down with my crises. Did they get worn down and tired of it? I knew they loved me and wanted me with them, and I wanted to be with them. But it was hard getting so very sick time after time. Whatever happened, I still hoped and wanted to be able to laugh and feel pleasure right up to the end of my days. I wanted my family to feel it too, to be able to laugh and joke and share fun times and enjoy being with me.

As I looked ahead at my empty calendar, there were no meetings, no expectations, just plenty of time to read and write. I didn't feel good enough to write letters, except I kept composing them in my head: a letter to show my concern for another cancer patient, a letter to a young man's mom who was worried about discouragement, a letter of thanks for a beautiful sweater sent by my friends in Mexico, a letter to a friend who had had a stroke. Perhaps I could write those overdue cards. But my penmanship was not very good writing from a reclining position. Concentration wasn't good either, and getting the supplies seemed difficult. I cajoled myself into thinking that I needed this time to rest and heal, and that it was OK just to read, rest and listen to music.

Nuts!

"Rest in the Lord, and wait patiently for Him." [Psalms 37:7 KJV]

After several weeks I went to Courage Center for physical therapy in the pool to restore my ability to walk. A therapist outlined a plan for exercises to help me regain strength and endurance. As I imitated her movements paddling with a stick that had a foam ball on either end, it hurt as I heard "pop." Another rib fractured. "Don't do that one," she said as she put my paddle down.

S-l-o-w-l-y I began getting better from the spinal fractures. I could be active enough to water a plant. I could walk the length of the hallway to the dining room. But eating made the brace uncomfortably tight and the walking made me breathless.

Accommodation

Cancer! Long term illness! Pain!

Hard, hard to live with!

Fighting? No! Fighting causes tension and that makes it worse.

Accommodation? Yes—making room for it, letting it slow me down, permitting it to temper my activities, making me think and ponder and meditate.

Good *years*? I guess they are gone now, have been gone for awhile. A year without problems is improbable.

Good *moments*? Oh yes! Hours, days, perhaps even *months* without new problems. They are here to savor, to enjoy, to hang on to, to share.

It was imperative for me to have devotion and prayer time at the beginning and end of each day. Unless I could put myself "in tune with God," I was discouraged. Problems piled up, interweaving and tangling. Hope for a "normal" life was not realistic. But I refused to consider it a sick life.

Not all of it was sick! I still enjoyed people very much. They were a tonic—all those hugs, words, casseroles and loaves of bread were full of love. I could smile. I could be grateful. I could enjoy! That was wellness. I could think and write and share.

> *My task had been simplified. When I remembered that the sole duty of human beings was to love God and fellow beings, I could react with love toward others. I did not understand its magic, but I received love in return.*

Pain

For years I had lectured at seminars about pain control. I thought I understood it. I was glad modern pharmacology had found combinations of drugs and modalities of treatment that could create an almost pain-free state, even with advanced disease. I felt a bit betrayed that my body reacted to most pain medications in a negative way.

The other very hard part of living with long-term illness was seeing its weight on my husband's shoulders, seeing his sagging puffy cheeks, his tearful bewildered eyes, his face with a scowl of worry lines. How could I help him? How could I give happiness to him? When he is weary of the weight and overwhelmed with responsibility, what could I do? Could I do something more effective than smiling and saying "thank you—I love you"? I felt helpless watching him in weariness and despair.

He loved the hymn "What a Friend We Have In Jesus." O, how I wish he'd permit Jesus to lift some of the load.

Rest in the Lord!

This time of extreme pain, disability and dependence was hard on both of us. We were both aware of that and tried very hard to stay hopeful, cheerful, undaunted, capable and upbeat. Most of the time we succeeded fairly well. We verbalized well to each other and to our friends with honesty and without bitterness. We admitted out loud and in quiet prayer our need for God's help. More than once, I found myself struggling to find my God of comfort. I didn't understand why the feeling was so elusive when I'd found it so many times in the past. The length and depth of this ordeal was a test of no small proportion.

From CANCER to cancer

"Turnabout is fair play," so goes the old saying. It didn't quite seem like fair play when Bill was diagnosed with cancer in the fall of 1991. During a routine yearly exam, Bill told of changes he had noticed in urination. Examination by palpation did not alarm either of the two doctors. The prostate gland was firm and enlarged, but smooth. It was at Bill's insistence that a blood test was taken. Results would be reported in a week. However, the next day the doctor called and told Bill to come back. The PSA blood test was ten times higher than normal. Ultrasound and biopsies were ordered. They showed conclusive evidence of aggressive, rapidly-growing prostate cancer that had extended beyond the gland, but had not metastasized. Surgery would not be sufficient to remove all the cancer cells. Radiation treatment was the best choice.

Bill wrote to his friends,

"Twenty years ago when Marvyl was diagnosed it was frightening; it was CANCER! We've lived with it for nearly 20 years and its now more like cancer. It's nothing new and not so frightening."

Eight weeks of radiation were medically uneventful. What did surprise Bill was the extreme fatigue and lassitude he felt. Having seen me experience it had not prepared him for experiencing the same reality. Radiation zaps more than cancer cells.

Bill also discovered an opportunity that enabled him to give, as well as receive, support. A pleasant, smiling friend named Howard, who lived in our complex, also had treatment at the same clinic. They asked to share treatment time so they could go together. Bonding and mutual respect developed. They went off together, a pair like Mutt and Jeff, for Howard was about half Bill's size.

Nevertheless, I sometimes worried. There were times when Bill was lethargic and refused to reach out. I remembered I went through several weeks or months of that, so I tried to show patience and understanding. He had to decide when he was ready to do more. His frowns, his sleepless nights and his desire for isolation bothered me. Yet, I was overwhelmed with gratitude for what he did so willingly for me because of my increasing disability. When we went to bed together, two hurting people, I had feelings of dismay, mingled with the feelings of gratitude and grace.

It was a low day when my neurologist and my oncologist confirmed that my brace would never be thrown away. I had hoped it was temporary. The anticipated course for the rest of my life would include frequent fractures and wearing the brace day and night. That night I woke up at 3 a.m. and could not get back to sleep.

Anger and dismay!

To quiet myself, I began to sing in my mind some of my favorite hymns:

"Breathe on me Breath of God, Fill me with life anew. . . Until with Thee I will one will, to do and to endure."

"O Master let me walk with thee......help me to bear the strain of toil, the fret of care."

"O teach me Lord that I may teach, the precious things Thou dost impart, and wing my words that they may reach, to hidden depths of many a heart."[11]

The next day I felt I needed somewhere to release my festering anger, frustration and disappointment about my brace and fragile bones. I asked Bill to take me to the cancer support group at the hospital. I talked and I listened. I found understanding in venting my anger, but surprisingly, I found I also gave. A young man with a brain tumor said as he was leaving, "I'd like to give you a hug." It wasn't sympathy; it was understanding and gratitude for things we had shared. Again, I was amazed how God conveyed His answers, if I would listen and believe.

Shall I give away my skis?

I asked my doctor, "Shall I give away my skis, or will I use them again?"

"Unless you *never* fall down, probably not."

"Will I walk or be able to straighten up without the brace?"

"Probably not."

"Will I drive again? Can we travel again?"

"Only if you do it lying down."

What a blessing we lived in a retirement community where meals and activities were planned for us, and friends were only a few steps away. We lived with new priorities, new limitations. BUT, WE WERE LIVING!

Bill and I both had work to do. Bill was taking the pictures of all residents and mounting them in cabinets he had made for the entrance way. We were working on the resident newsletter, learning to run a computer, playing games, singing in the choir. I was doing a lot of writing and editing for the American Cancer Society, planning some workshops and attending others. Love and faithfulness to each other and from God kept us unafraid and content. Not long ago I said, "I'm glad I'm old enough so I'll never have to learn the confusing mysteries of a computer." Now Bill and I had to bargain for time to use it. Our computer-knowledgeable son, Paul, came weekly to bail me out of the confusing mazes I got myself into. My grandchildren summed it up nicely:

"Eric, I bet you understand more about computers than I do," I said.

"Of course I do, Grandma, I learned that in kindergarten and now I'm in first grade."

To Mara, who was eight, I said, "You know we did not have computers when I went to school."

She replied, "I'm sorry, Grandma, that's too bad, but it just can't be helped!"

So I had to learn.

The time came for Bill's evaluation with his doctor. The treatment was successful in reducing the cancer growth although the doctors were certain it would return in time.

"Perhaps one year, perhaps 30 years from now," said the doctor.

"I will go for the 30," Bill replied.

"Good," said the doctor, "I'm recording that on your chart."

Loving Inspiration

It was so easy to find inspiration from watching our grandchildren. Little David came running to me with arms outstretched. "I love you," he said, as I stooped to hug him and he patted the top of *my* head. He felt that was part of hugging. Later the whole family sat around the table playing a game. With deliberate purpose, David worked his way around the table, sitting on each adult lap, soaking up love and giving it as well. The response of each person to love is so wonderful. Why does mankind not do it all the time, everywhere? Jesus Christ came to show us that is the way God wants us to live. Not in judgment, criticism or hate, but to live with love, acceptance and appreciation of each other. Life is wonderful when we do that. How come we've almost lost the way?

Looking around, I was amazed at the good people who so often get no attention in the media, which usually presents only the sensational. Not everyone has been blessed with sheer energy to do great things. Some are devout in their prayers, or quietly spread love by little notes, fresh bread and warm hugs.

A book for cancer patients

Service and Rehabilitation was a committee of the American Cancer Society with which I had been active for many years. In 1987 the program director for cancer care at University of Minnesota Hospitals asked for someone from American Cancer Society to help with the development of a booklet for cancer patients, I volunteered. Specialists, therapists, social workers and nurses wrote some information that was uniformly applicable. I selected and condensed information from the many American Cancer Society pamphlets. My committee members and I wrote pages of information. To make the book more "user friendly," several people submitted appealing little sketches. Our goal was to lessen fear and help people understand treatment.

We were pleased when the National American Cancer Society credited our work with an Honors Citation. But we noticed a significant limitation: our book was not useful for many who recently came to this country, ethnic minorities and others who had a low level of English literacy. They were known as the "underserved" in terms of health care. It was our goal to let them know where to go for help. Not only were these people unable to understand English, but in their native country there was no understanding, nor availability, of care for cancer. In most "third world" countries there is no such thing as cancer treatment. We questioned missionaries from Africa, refugees from Asia and nurses who worked in the hospitals. In 1992 teachers in English as a Second Language, staff from the State Department of Education and from the Society for the Blind were on the committee who spent hours revising the *Cancer Information Handbook.*[12] Long sentences and long words in the first book were shortened and the type enlarged for the new book, *Cancer Help for You and Your Family.*[12] We researched literature and found an especially good resource in *Ethics Variations in Dying, Death and Grief,*[13] which developed as a result of a series of multi-ethnic workshops.

New Years 1992

I haven't written in my journal during the busy holidays. Where am I spiritually, physically and emotionally at this new beginning? Kind of jumbled. Kind of joyful. Kind of tired. Not quite satisfied, not thoroughly happy with myself and my condition. I think of joy—joy because God fills my heart and my motives with love. Great joy that my Bill is loving and well. Great joy that my children are so attentive and show so much care and love. Great joy that my grandchildren are so beautiful, so whole, so promising, so full of loving ways.

Having pain for a long time was not easy. I tried to relate it to Christ's pain. His was certainly greater—but it did not last so long. I knew God was loving, but how come He allowed so much pain and suffering. Not just mine, but the hungry waifs we saw in Mexico, the people in the Philippines devastated by a typhoon, those people under the oppression of uncaring despots, the disease and filth in overcrowded countries. How come, God? If that isn't the way you want it to be, how come You allow it.

Did I feel God's grace? Since my broken back and that horrible experience with pain medication, I had to reach more, search more to find it. It was not so automatic—that feeling that God was near and guiding. It was disappointing to have that spontaneous certainty gone. Would I regain it? How had I and the rest of the world gotten so out of hand, out of the hand of God? The theological and political questions were too complicated for me. Unless I remembered to simply trust, it was very discouraging. What did God want? Only trust in Him and loving relationships with all I meet? That's about all I could do. But, I *could* do that!

March 1993

My brace irritates, both at my shoulders and around my abdomen. It digs into my neck and chin and presses on my stomach—Infection in the bronchi hurts my chest, my throat— I have no voice—A good friend died last night—

Living to the hilt, feeling high with the highs and down with the tragedies, is that the way to get the most out of life? I am feeling "blah," like who cares? That's not me.

I envy my 80- and 90-year-old friends who still live with vigorous healthy bodies. A healthy life style has always been mine. I always valued it and never abused it. My body was never a perfect "10," but most of the time it did what I wanted it to do. Well, it was never a beautiful diver or dancer and it never won contests, but it served me well. It was strong and enduring and functional.

God, am I really able to serve you better with all these restrictions?

Determination and enthusiasm have gotten me far in life. They've helped me overcome shyness and uncertainty. Has the time come for me to hear other voices: like Acquiescence and Boundaries? "No's" instead of "yes's"? "Acceptance" instead of "Try"?

I had a birthday: 70. A good age to be. When I was 50, I thought I was still young. The process of aging and cancer over the last 20 years has convinced me I'm not. These years are described as "the freedom years." We are described as "chronologically advantaged," in the "golden years." The month of May had been nationally declared as "Older American's Month." I was asked to write something for a compilation of senior writings. I could not find my poetic muse. I thought a long while about life's meaningful experiences and about the disabilities of the last two years. Quite suddenly, an allegorical poem overflowed from my mind to pen and page:

OLD AGE: A SEA LIFE ALLEGORY

I think of the moon jelly fish,
Its convoluted edges pulsing in and out, in and out
As it wanders at random
In a sea of nutrients rich in variety and availability.

I think of a feisty crab,
Traveling crossways in the main stream,
Its horny claws grasping
Open jaws voraciously chewing.

I think of a few gaudy trigger fish,
Their bright colors and garish make-up
Not hiding their age or position.
Do they really think it does?

I think of the staid loggerhead sponge,
Tough, locked in one place,
Not being moved by time nor tide
So the depths of its recesses are never known.

No longer caught up in busy schools,
Whose synchronistic movements,
Sudden shifts of attention and changes of direction,
Are so spectacular to behold.

No longer gracefully enchanting,
Like dolphins and porpoises, leaping and playing,
Their gentle smiles and trusting manner
Reflecting the innocence of childhood.

No longer like sharks on their sinister patrols,
Swerving back and forth, back and forth,
Taking advantage of other's weaknesses,
Causing terror with their indomitable power.

No longer like tantalizing octopi,
Able to change shape and color to match any environment,
Able to squeeze into any locale where they want to be,
Quickly accomplishing the seemingly impossible.

Yes, more like the moon jelly fish,
Many tenuous strings still dangling
But no longer needing to go anyplace,
Nor needing to hurry, nor make an impact.

Satisfied with simplicity, but with definite rhythm.
Pulse, pulse, out, in, out, in
More than a ghost, more than a shadow—
Somewhat fragile, somewhat beautiful, somewhat transparent.

People watch, but not to capture the ephemeral jelly fish.
There is no great demand for whatever it has to offer,
Yet it floats in the sea of life, not demanding, not pushing
Just enjoying being present amidst creation.

© *Marvyl Patton*

I needed to listen to its message. Although it came from my mind, I needed to believe its truth to find solace and serenity. Was that strange? No, the pep talks we all need from time to time can come from either inside or outside the self.

The "teacher-preacher" part of me said "don't quit."
The "follower-listener" part of me said "relax and enjoy." Which voice, God, should I pay attention to? I'm listening. Doors were slamming shut and others opening. Which one was I to enter?

We need the mountain tops
to give us vision,
but we travel the farthest
in the valleys.

Accept them,
for both are a part of life.

14

Leap of Faith

This is the most important chapter in my book. Without this one, none of the other chapters could have been written.

God has many ways of reaching us as His children. How He reaches us and speaks to us depends on where we are geographically, historically and personally. Throughout the history of mankind, there has always been a reaching towards a higher power. All cultures have searched to find a supreme being. Not one of us as human beings is as great as our Creator.

To be heard by God, or to listen to Him, my personal orientation needs no shaman, nor wise old man, nor inner child, no hierarchy of spirits or saints. How does God speak to man? Fr. John Powell's book says, "God speaks through the portals of our minds, our will, our imagination, our memory and our emotion."[2] I think He also speaks through the wonders of nature, through the deeds and words of other people. If I am tuned in to Him, I feel His love and His guidance in many ways, and I feel a peaceful sense of security.

The father of the sick child in Mark 9:24 said, "O Lord, I believe. Help Thou my unbelief." The noted theologian, Soren Kirkegaard, coined the phrase "leap of faith" as the step necessary to bridge the gap. Knowledge and logic provided solid ground up to the brink of the chasm. But still there remained mysteries unsolved, happenings unexplained and evidence that defied testing. It was necessary to leap the chasm to get to the other side where faith gives greater understanding. That leap carried me over to God as a personal heavenly Father. When I acted on that belief, it led me down paths I didn't know were there.

To find God, I had to LEAP.

Some people have said to me, "If you just have enough faith you can be cured." Why did they think that? The Bible is full of accounts of people of faith who were not spared from thorns, pain, disease and suffering. Even the Son of God was not spared. There were greater miracles in the help of God to live with these challenges than if the problems were swept away. Belief in a loving heavenly Father does not protect me from troubles and death, but many times faith in God transformed a painful experience into a beautiful one. It has transformed fear to peace, suffering to gratitude. Faith has made a difference.

Quotations, Biblical or from people living today, were such powerful guidelines, different ones all the time. "Be strong and of good courage" was a Biblical message I needed often when I was wallowing, when I didn't feel good, when I didn't feel encouraged, and didn't feel like encouraging anyone else. I was indeed subject to all the usual "bugs" that affected most of the population, but I was able to bounce back from both the disease and the depression by letting mind and medicine help the body heal.

In regard to some current writings about illness as a metaphor, illness as a response to a misdirected life, illness as a reason to change to another way, illness as a maladaptive response to a negative situation, I want to defend every patient, myself included! I have never felt my life was misdirected. Through my faith, my training and my experience, I always felt divine presence and divine guidance, if I but looked for it, asked for it and trusted it.

> *If illness redirected my life, it was not because I was off track, but because I was receiving opportunity to serve in new ways.*

I've always felt that part of my ability to understand and serve cancer patients was because I was there myself.

I don't really know, nor think it important to know, whether my illness is a genetic predisposition, a hazardous exposure, a stressful time, a God-given, Satan-given, man-given or self-given disease. All I need to understand is that it is here and brings certain limitations and experiences. With God I can find the strength, wisdom, help and patience to fulfill a purpose and strive toward a goal. I resent the implication that places blame on others or on myself. Our very humanness includes imperfection and the need of each human to receive help from both God and fellow man.

It was a time of realization for me, of facing squarely the permanence of my injured bones. The neurological specialist said my brace would always be necessary for the rest of my life. I had hoped it would be a temporary thing, that in 8 weeks, 10 weeks, 15 weeks, with exercise

and healing, I would take it off. My limits and endurance with a damaged spine went beyond what I expected. It changed nearly every aspect of my life from
what I wore morning and night, to where I went, what
I did, even what I ate. I reacted by being discouraged
and with overdoing laughter. I was defiant. I was not
going to let this defeat nor depress me. I was going to
enjoy the people, the moments, the activities.

I put arms around my neighbor, Paula, as together
we watched the others take down the Christmas deco-
rations. Her built-up shoe and her limp, my brace and
my posture were there for always, but we would not let
it cause us to enjoy life less. How intertwined we were
to one another, all of us.

We are often unaware how significant our helpfulness is. Three people sought me out last week just to tell
me of biopsies and tests that concerned them. I could
not change nor cure any of them, yet somehow my
listening, my relating to them gave them strength and
hope. That did not come *from* me; it came from God
through me. How blessed to be a vehicle to transport His
love. How strangely powerful such moments were.

I didn't like the over-solicitousness of those who
offered pity or pushed scriptural healing, or who didn't
understand long-term illness. I felt it was my faith that
had sustained me and given me a good life despite
continuous disease. That was a miracle, too. When I
looked back, I could hardly believe I had lived this way
for 20 years, with serious life-threatening cancer, pain
and side effects too numerous to count.

And yet I felt I'd had a good life, good health, good
times.

Faith in God had helped me live with cancer,
struggle with uncertainties and accept my body's limitations.

Faith in family and friends helped, loving with warmth and presence; sharing the frustrations, the doubts and especially the joys.

Faith in self helped, realizing that what I did and what I felt was up to my choosing. My attitude toward the people and the happenings in my life affected the outcome.

Faith in medical care helped, especially physicians who realized we were a team and that we needed to share knowledge to achieve a goal.

Lack of faith in any of those areas weakened the chances for a good outcome. By attending first to Faith in God, all the others were added to it.

Faith!
Faith in God.
Faith in self.
Faith in family and friends.
Faith in the medical advisors!

It was important for me to spend time worshipping God, reading Scripture and pondering thoughts of other believers. That was especially true when I'd wake up from a hurting night to face another day of discomfort, and it seemed all I could do was lie in bed, aware of my sick body.

Or is that all I can do? Had I another choice?

I could take out my books, or my tape recorder, or turn on the radio. I could deliberately choose to pay attention to those faithful believers in God and in Jesus. I could soak my mind and spirit in thoughts of hope and gratefulness. I could do this until, inside my body, the heart that seemed to be quivering in uncertainty, felt calm again. Until the pain that occupied my back and abdomen lessened. It happened when I gave myself over to listening and realizing the power of God.

The right passage sometimes seemed to leap out of what I was reading or hearing.

If I chose, I could think again about the doubts, hurts and suffering, but why do that? I had found a way out. The thoughts and faith of others helped me find my faith and peace again.

What had I to offer from my days and years of living with cancer? Was there anything unique or inspiring in my experiences that I could share? What could I tell others to help them? What kind of telling helped me? Was it the teaching kind? Poetry? Sermons? Lectures? Education? All of these from time to time. I gobbled up education to understand the ways of my body. I reveled in, relaxed with, poets who said so much in just a few words. There were sermons that stood out in my memory as directions. But mostly, it was true stories from other people that helped me find answers. I, too, wanted to be a witness of hope and care to others who were hurting and doubtful.

The unique part was that I had lived so long with so many complications and that I believed faith in God had helped me do that with more joy than sorrow, more beauty than anguish.

> *Acquiring knowledge had given me confidence, removed fear. Relationships, not isolation, had given me comfort.*

Go tell everyone, says the Scripture. Who wants to hear? That was not my question to answer. The Bible just said, "Go tell."

God has shown me that His strength is sufficient in all circumstances. He has sustained me in the hazard-filled valley of disease for more than twenty years. He has given me surprising high points on the mountains.

"Rejoice evermore.... Pray without ceasing.... In everything give thanks." [I Thessalonians 5:16-18].
What did those words mean to me?
A brace encircles my body and limits all my movements. It is hot and inhibiting. I used to get relief from tension by getting on my knees in the garden, digging in the dirt with my bare hands, extracting wonder from observing the process of growth from small seed to flower. If I think about what I cannot do, I would feel dejected, maybe bitter.

BUT—

I still plant flowers in pots on the deck, watch their growth, care for those whipped and dried by wind, water those scorched by sun, encourage those that are tiny and overshadowed. Through a magnifier I see intricacies and beauties hidden, note a rhythm of life, am awed by diversity of form. I am even amazed at the fat succulent body and tiny legs of the mealy bug I try so hard to get rid of.

To which do I give the most attention?

I listen to the news. Strife, discord, killings in neighborhoods and between nations. Confusion and failure in governments. I listen and feel discouraged and scared by the inhumanity and the way the world is living.

BUT—

I receive a touch on the shoulder from a friend. I witness the dedication of the workers at the food shelf. I see my husband give his special skills as a lawyer to aid a friend in a nursing home. I hear a young voice on the phone say, "I love you, Grandma." I exchange thoughts with a friend. The bowl on the table is full of cards of love and care. I hear my children calling me and coming to be with me.

> To which do I give the most attention?
> Whatsoever things are lovely—?

Malignancy and degeneration consume my body.
    Others, equally wounded, hold my hand and I hold theirs.

Few, if any of us, have life with no adversity.
    We can despair at the tragedy—or exult in the challenge.
    We can cry with hopelessness—or pray with hope.
    We can moan over our fate—or we can ask God for guidance.

Therein lies the difference.

The choice belongs to each one of us.

Glossary

Allopurinal = a medication used to aid the body to prevent the build up of uric acid and waste products.

American Cancer Society = an organization of volunteers and health professionals that provides education, service and research relating to cancer.

Angiogram = injection of a dye into the blood stream so it may be visualized by X-ray and studied by the doctor.

Betadine = an antiseptic solution used to cleanse the skin.

Bifurcation = the point at which a vein or artery divides into two channels.

Biopsy = removal of body tissue for microscopic examination.

Bird's nest = a filter surgically placed in the vena cava (major vein) to catch blood clots and prevent them from traveling to heart and lungs.

Cartilaginous tissue = the tough, elastic connective tissue that is part of the skeleton.

Catheter = a slender rubber or plastic hollow tube inserted in a part of the body for draining or instilling fluids.

CT or CAT scan = means Computerized Axial Tomography, which by means of many X-rays creates a detailed picture of internal parts of the body for medical study.

Chemotherapy = a type of medication given for a disease such as cancer; may be given in a variety of ways—by mouth, injection, implant of a pump, intravenous drip, etc.

Colostomy = a surgically-created opening made in the abdomen for release of bowel contents when the bowel is diseased and cannot function normally.

Coumadin = medication given to "thin" the blood or decrease the incidence of unwanted clots in the blood stream.

Cytomel = brand name for a synthetic form of thyroid hormone.

Diverticulitis = inflammative of small pouch-like swellings in the colon or elsewhere in the digestive tract.

Electromyogram = a test which uses electrical impulses to detect normalities in the function of muscles.

Embolism = a clot of blood that lodges in a blood vessel and restricts normal flow.

EMG = abbreviation for electromyogram

Enterostomal therapist = a nurse who has special training in the care and functioning of stomas created to replace malfunctioning parts of the colon, intestines or bladder.

Fentanyl patch = a pain medication applied by a skin patch and released slowly into the body.

Fluoroscope = a type of X-ray machine that projects a picture on a screen and allows a doctor to study the internal body in motion.

Gallium scan = a test where certain radio-active particles are injected into the body where they concentrate in certain areas indicating the presence of disease.

Gastroenterologist = a doctor who specializes in the study and treatment of the digestive tract, especially the stomach and the bowel.

Gastrograph = a study of stomach function

Hematological = relating to processes of the blood stream.

Hematoma = a blood-filled swelling

Heparin = a liquid substance injected under the skin or into a vein which goes into the blood stream and prevents unwanted clots from forming.

Hyperthyroidism = presence of too much thyroxin, a colorless hormone that regulates growth; secreted by the thyroid gland.

ICC = I Can Cope - a series of educational classes for cancer patients and family members.

Imagery = an exercise of using mental pictures to reduce stress and relieve pain.

Ischemia = poor blood supply to the bowel, heart or other part of the body.

IV = intravenous = a method of injecting medication or nutrition directly into the blood stream.

Lin-ac = abbreviated way of saying linear accelerator, which is a high-energy X-ray machine for treating some kinds of cancer.

Make Today Count (MTC) = an organized support group for people with any chronic disease that threatens or alters life.

Metastasis = spread of cancer cells from the site of origin to another location in the body.

Nasal gastric tube (NG tube) = a flexible hollow tube inserted through the nose into the stomach to suction out a build up of gas or excess fluid that cannot escape via the intestine.

Oncologist = a doctor who specializes in the study and treatment of cancer.

Orthostatic = intensified drop in blood pressure which occurs when person goes from prone or sitting position to standing.

Orthotist = a person who specializes in making braces or artificial body parts to help correct a defect.

Ostomy = a surgically-created body opening as an alternative route when disease prevents normal function. For example: Urostomy = opening in the abdomen for a diseased bladder; colostomy for a diseased colon, ileostomy for a diseased small intestine, and in the neck, laryngectomy, for a diseased larynx (voice box).

Pacemaker = a device placed under the skin and connected to the heart by a metal wire to give electrical impulses to control heart beat.

PAS port = Peripheral Access System, a device placed in the forearm and used for the administration of fluids and medication into a vein. A similar device called a Port A Cath is placed in the chest wall for the same purpose.

Peristalsis = wave-like movements of the intestine (or other hollow organs) that propel nutrients along for absorption and elimination.

Petechiae = small pinpoint hemorrhages under the skin, resulting in purple to red spots and streaks.

Phlebotomist = a person skilled and trained in the drawing of blood.

Physiatrist = a medical doctor specializing in physical medicine or the way muscles of the body work.

PRN = abbreviation which means give medication as needed.

Poorly differentiated cells = cells that are abnormal in appearance and do not closely resemble the cells in the organ from which they come. They may be irregular in shape, too large, too small, with a membrane too thick or too thin, or a nucleus that is too large or too small, etc.

Proctitis = inflammation of the membranes in the rectum.

PSA blood test = analysis of a blood sample to measure the Prostate Specific Antigens which are elevated in prostate cancer or certain other conditions of the prostate gland.

PTT = Partial pro-Thrombin Time, a blood test to detect clotting time when heparin is used to control clot formation.

Pulmonary embolism = a blood clot that moves from its place of origin into the lungs and restricts normal flow of blood from heart to lungs.

Saphenous vein = a large vein in the leg which is just under the skin surface.

Sparine = a medication

Spondylolithesis = spinal vertebrae slip out of place, resulting in misalignment and distortion of the back.

Stoma = a mouth-like opening in plants or animals.

Syncope = fainting

Tachycardia = heartbeat that is too rapid.

TEDS = thigh-high anti-embolism stockings

TENS = Transcutaneous Electrical Nerve Stimulation, a device which sends electrical impulses through the skin to the nerves to lessen pain and to stimulate healing.

Thrombocytopenia = a condition of too few platelets (which promote clotting) in the blood stream which causes uncontrolled and excessive bleeding.

Ultrasound = use of high-frequency sound waves to locate and study differences in tissue density.

Vascular = pertaining to the blood vessels.

Vasculation = delivery of blood and blood products to body parts.

Bibliography

1. Johnson, Judi, and Klein, Linda. *I Can Cope*, Second edition, Minneapolis, MN: CROMIMED, 1994. Page 59.
2. Powell, John, S.J. *He Touched Me*, Allen, TX: Tabor Publishing, ©1974. Quoted by permission. Page 79.
3. Weatherhead, Leslie. *The Will of God*, 1944, Nashville, TN: Abington Press, Copyright renewed 1972. Quoted by permission. Page 93.
4. Baker, Russell. *Growing Up*, New York, NY: Congdon and Weed, 1982. Quoted by permission. Page 96.
5. Schuler, Robert S. *Hour of Power Choral Responses*, Fred Bock Music Co., Alexander, IN: Alexander House, 1977. Used by permission. Page 156.
6. Frankl, Viktor. *Man's Search for Meaning*, New York: Washington Square Press, 1963. Page 181.
7. Kidd, Sue Monk. *When God Whispers*, Carmel, NY: Guideposts. Page 183.
8. Al-Anon Family Group. *Day at a Time in Al-Anon*, New York: 1981. Page 191.
9. Lewis, C. S. *Letters to Malcom, Chiefly on Prayer*, New York, NY: Harcourt Brace and Janovich, Inc., 1964. Page 192.
10. Brandt, Leslie. *Psalms Now*, Concordia Publishing House, 1973. Page 195.
11 *Pilgrim Hymnal, The*, Boston, Mass: Pilgrim Press, 1959. Hatch, Edwin. *Church Psalter and Hymn Book*, 1954. P. 218. Words by Washington Gladden; Words by Frances Havergal, Words by Joseph Scriven. Quoted by permission.
12. Minnesota Division of the American Cancer Society, Minneapolis, MN.
    Cancer and the Elderly, Page 108.
    Mutual Help Facilitators Manual. Page 181.
    Cancer Information Handbook for Patients and Family, 1989. Page 221.
    Cancer Help for You and Your Family, 1993. Page 221.
13. Irish, Donald P., Lundquist, Kathleen F., and Nelson, Vivian Jenkins. *Ethnic Variations in Dying, Death and Grief*, Bristol, PA: Taylor and Francis, 1993. (Compiled from conference speakers at the Minnesota Coalition for Death Education and Support.) Page 221.

Index

To Order Copies

If unavailable in local bookstores, LangMarc will fill your order within 24 hours.

(**Telephone Orders:** Call 1-800-864-1648

✉ **Postal Orders:** LangMarc Publishing, P.O. 33817
San Antonio, TX 78265-3817. USA.

Guide-Lines and God-Lines For Facing Cancer
Soft cover $13.95

Quantity Discounts: 10% discount for 3-4 copies; 15% for 5-9 copies; 20% for 10 or more copies.
Shipping: Send check with your order, and shipping is free. For phone orders, add Book Rate $1.50 for first book; 50 cents for each additional book. For Priority or UPS: $3.00 for 1-2 books; 50 cents for each additional book.
Sales tax: Texas residents only, add 7.25% ($1.00).
Send a Gift to a Friend: We will mail directly. Shipping cost to each address will be $3.00 UPS or $1.50 Book Rate.

Please send payment with order.

_____ books @ $13.95: _____

Sales tax (Texas res. only): _____

Shipping: _____

Check enclosed: _____

Name and Address for order delivery:

Thank you for your order.